A China More Just

Gao Zhisheng rose from utter poverty to become one of China's most acclaimed lawyers and a leading advocate for the oppressed. Life took a most unlikely turn in 1991 when Gao happened to learn, while selling vegetables by the roadside, that the country was looking to train new lawyers. Though he possessed only a middle-school education, Gao taught himself law and passed the national bar examination in 1995.

Gao made headlines in 1999 by winning the largest medical malpractice lawsuit in Chinese history. In 2001, China's Ministry of Justice named him one of the nation's top ten attorneys. A Christian, Gao has since become known for his tenacious pursuit of justice on behalf of China's most vulnerable—from exploited coal miners to democracy advocates, the poor, and victims of religious persecution.

In 2005 Gao wrote a series of open letters to China's authorities detailing his investigation into the torture of members of Falun Gong. Thereafter he found himself "besieged," as he put it, by infuriated communist rulers.. Gao's Beijing law firm was soon after shut down, his family put under surveillance, and attempts made on his life. In 2006 he initiated a series of hunger strikes that involved thousands worldwide.

Gao's maltreatment by the Chinese regime has been the subject of formal resolutions by the United States Congress and the European Parliament. Rights groups such as Amnesty International have campaigned to ensure his welfare. He has been featured by *The New York Times*, *Washington Post*, *The Guardian*, and many other prominent media.

In 2006 Gao became the recipient of the Chinese Liberal Culture Movement's Special Human Rights Award, the Asia-Pacific Human Rights Foundation's Human Rights Champion Award, and in 2007 was awarded the American Board of Trial Advocates' Courageous Advocacy Award. He is a Nobel Peace Prize nominee.

A China More Just

My Fight as a Rights Lawyer in the World's Largest Communist State

BROAD
PRESS

BROAD PRESS USA

FIRST ENGLISH-LANGUAGE EDITION

This is a translation of the Chinese-language text, *Shen Yu Women Bingjian Zuozhan*, published in 2006 by Broad Press, here abridged and updated.

This book was made possible through the generous support of the International Intellectual Fund.

Printed in Taiwan R.O.C.

Broad Press USA
6755 Mira Mesa Blvd. #123-189
San Diego, CA 92121, USA
editor@broadpressinc.com

For distribution and order inquiries:
Tel: 1-888-268-2698
Fax: 1-866-759-2913
www.broadbook.com/english

ISBN: 1-932674-36-5

Cover design by www.3lotusmedia.co.uk

Contents

三 Advocating for Rights

四 Open Letters for Justice

五 The Siege on My Family: A Journal

Preface

"It is our misfortune to live in the China of this historical period. No one on this earth has ever had to experience or witness the suffering that has befallen us! Yet it is also our fortune to live in the China of this historical period. For we will experience and witness how the greatest people on earth banished this suffering once and for all!"

Such were my concluding remarks on December 21, 2005, offered as stinging tears rolled down my cheeks when I addressed fellow citizens who had come to Beijing to petition the government.

I have never been a man of letters, and so it never occurred to me that I would write a book—much less in times as stifling as these.

In this time when the majority of my fellow Chinese have become numb to, or have even adapted to, the darkness and fallacies of this age, my writings have sparked hatred and fear in those despots who operate in the shadows. When the passion, the edge, and the righteous indignation that mark some of my words (in particular those exposing the infuriating wickedness of this dictatorship) at times pierce through the thick darkness enshrouding my fellow citizens, they—having long since grown acclimated to, or been forced to acclimate to, the darkness—may find the light of my words unsettling. This suggests that I have failed to "acclimate" to the national psyche of China. So be it.

This era is not just about enduring setbacks, however. We also have our share of achievements in this day. For me, someone with merely eight years of formal education, it is an achievement to have written something others want to read, and even more so to see it published in book form.

It's really not that I am fond of heaviness. But insofar as my writing is undeniably "heavy," it is because the weight, the burden, that I feel forces me to think and compels me to act, to pick up my pen. I must narrate this story. I am moved by an ardent hope that by articulating it, I may in some way help to relieve China of the crushing burden on her back.

Strictly speaking, I should be counted as an activist, not a thinker; much less am I the founder of some institution. I have sought in my writing a style that delights in its uninhibitedness and that speaks directly from the heart. Much of my writing is improvisational and spurred by circumstance. I myself am surprised at times by the roughness that marks it. Whatever the case, these are words that tell a tale both of the people's violent, sanguinary, bitter pain, as well as of the noble character, dignity, and resoluteness of the freedom fighters who are counted among them. Yet no words, however strong, can possibly describe the darkness and terrible barbarity of today's dictators in China, nor the tragic annihilation of Chinese culture that they have perpetrated. Though I have strived to convey these qualities through my writing, having attempted to unveil merely one corner of China's darkness, I cannot help but feel the futility and frailty of language.

In today's China, where the forces of incivility run rampant, it is common practice to mock what is beautiful and to beautify what is vile. A pathological China is not ready for what I write. But I hope such a China will soon emerge.

It is my sincerest wish that soon a China will exist where there is no need for chronicling such as mine.

Gao Zhisheng
Beijing, China

About This Book

This is a translation of the Chinese-language text, *Shen Yu Women Bingjian Zuozhan*, published in 2006 by Broad Press Inc., here abridged and updated. It is a selection of writings that includes essays, journal entries, and open letters.

The romanization system used in this translation is Pinyin. Most letters of the Pinyin alphabet are similar in pronunciation to their English counterparts, with a few notable exceptions:

Pinyin	English Equivalent
c	ts – as in "its"
q	ch – as in "chick"
ui	way – as in "sway"
x	sh – as in "shin"
zh	j – as in "john"

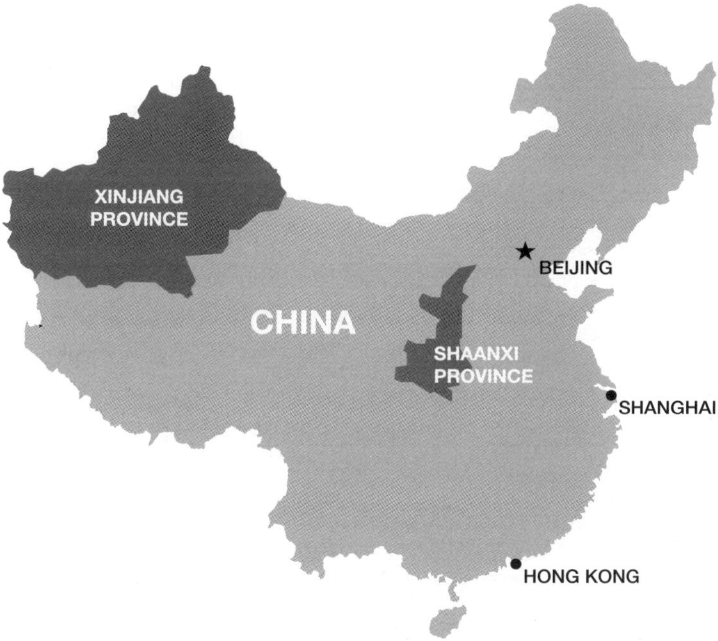
XINJIANG
PROVINCE
BEIJING
CHINA
SHAANXI
PROVINCE
SHANGHAI
HONG KONG

一

Growing Up Tender Yet Strong

I. From Peasant Child to Respected Attorney

"When will we ever have enough to eat?"

I was born in 1964 in the countryside of northern Shaanxi province. Chinese people were poor in those days, but our family was even poorer than most. I remember my father often sitting beside the cooking pit and grumbling to himself, "When will we ever have enough to eat?"

My father passed away when I was only ten. We had no money during his stay in the hospital. After he died, they wouldn't let us have the body because our family owed the hospital ten dollars.[1] That was a lot of money back then. But we were fortunate in that my schoolteacher's older brother, who was a local Party Secretary, helped by agreeing to

1 Here and throughout the book, the Chinese currency (the Yuan) has been converted to U.S. dollars for the reader's convenience. Measures of length, area, weight, etc., have been converted to miles, acres, tons, and so on. (This and all other footnotes are the editor's insertions.)

be our guarantor to the hospital. In the end we were able to take my father's body home.

From then on, our family had nothing. There were seven children in the family, with the oldest being seventeen and the youngest two. Once my older brothers and sisters reached around fourteen or fifteen years old, they were expected to go out and fend for themselves. In my adult years I asked my mother, "Why did you send us out at such an early age?" She replied simply that she thought we would have a better chance of survival away from the family, as we could have starved to death had she kept us together.

The year after our father died, my younger brother and I used to wander the mountains hunting for medicinal herbs to sell to feed the family. We would sell them at the local market held once every ten days. Each time the market rolled around, we would need to make enough money for the family to live on for the next ten days. My brother and I worked this way for two years.

When I turned fifteen, my brother and I got part-time jobs working as coal miners at the Huangling Coal Mine in Shaanxi. Now, whenever I learn of a coal mine accident, it reminds me of the conditions we once worked under. Society today pays attention when mining accidents occur and urges the employers to do something, but in those days such accidents were usually just dismissed. The death of a human being back then was considered about as important as the death of an ant.

Although we had part-time jobs, we earned almost nothing. We started out earning thirteen cents for each pile of coal we pulled up the hill, which was three-quarters of a mile long. The locals could afford to hire a mule to pull their loads, but we had to lug ours ourselves. We were the youngest of all the workers, yet also the weakest. The most we could pull was seventeen piles a day.

My heart would race every time someone shouted in the mining tunnel. And I also worried that my brother would be pushed around. If someone bullied me I was usually numb to it. But I was anxious for my brother.

The best moment of the day for us came when the number of piles we had lugged was tallied up and recorded on the mine wall. After nine months the wall was covered with markings. Ultimately, though, the most important thing was that we both came out of the mining ordeal alive.

One time a landslide crushed my brother's leg. The bone was broken and visible. I responded by searching frantically for old newspapers, burning them and pressing the ashes into my brother's wound. As I carried my brother out of the tunnel that day, I didn't think of bringing him to the hospital, but hoped only that the foreman could look after him for a time until he healed. When we approached the foreman he said merely that we had eaten too much over the past nine months and that he wouldn't give us a cent for our work. He then told us to leave. Things were trying for us then. Books today often say that in the "old China"[2] poor people were worse off than animals. That was certainly true for us, but this was 1980.

I didn't know what to do. I carried my brother to a cave dwelling that wasn't occupied. That evening we were discovered by the cave's owners—a farmer and his wife. The farmer asked, "Are you thieves?" We didn't respond to that, nor to his many other questions. We felt as good as dead. The farmer's wife was kindly and suggested that the farmer stop questioning us. It seemed she could tell we were just two miserable kids. She told us that we could stay in their cave. They left and returned

2 A term commonly used to refer to China before the Communist Party took power in 1949.

a half hour later with some food for us. Thinking back, I bet even pigs wouldn't have eaten that food.

The farmer was a small man. While we were eating he asked if I would be willing to work for him. I immediately agreed to do so as long as he would feed us. He explained that they too were poor, so he couldn't afford to feed my brother. But he promised to pay me nine cents a day.

Nine cents back then could buy two big bags of biscuits. I worked daily for a month and always asked the farmer to buy two bags of biscuits for, and bring water for, my brother. I went to work before sunrise each day and returned after it was completely dark. The first thing I did on returning was to go to my brother, feel his body temperature and make sure he was still breathing.

In only one month's time, and having received no medical treatment, my brother miraculously healed. Poor people are uncannily resilient.

After he became well, I planned to have him stay with our older brother in Xi'an. I needed to stay behind to go see a former employer for whom I had repaired bridges; he owed me five dollars and fifty cents.

The farmer borrowed two dollars from someone and gave it to me to buy a bus ticket for my brother. As my brother and I parted, we cried heartily. We were both at a loss for words then, especially me. I didn't know if I would ever see him again.

I continued to work for the farmer for twenty days to pay him back. After that I decided to stay for another week to help him remake the dirt floor of his cave. As I prepared to leave he hugged me and said tearily, "You're a good kid. You could have just taken the two dollars and left, and even then we wouldn't have resented you for it. But you didn't do that, and you even worked more for us!"

I had only two plans in mind for myself, as my thinking was quite simple back then. The first was to get the five dollars and fifty cents owed to me, and the second was to enlist in the army. My older brother had been a soldier for three years, and I had heard that the troops ate well. I hoped that becoming a soldier might change my life for the better.

Twenty-five miles lay between the cave where I was living and the place from which I was to get my past wages. I went to that place every two or three days but always returned disappointed. Eventually I had to give up. I decided to set out for home, having no money.

The Winding Road Home

I began my journey home literally step by step… I walked twenty-five miles straight the first day and arrived in Huangling county starving; I hadn't eaten anything the whole way. As I passed a cafeteria I saw someone deep frying dough sticks. The eleventh month in the lunar calendar had arrived and it was winter. Cold as it was, the hunger that wrenched my stomach was even worse. I took off my old, worn-out coat and offered it to the owner, saying, "I'm almost starved to death. Could I trade this jacket for two fried dough sticks, please?" The man, who was middle-aged, grabbed me by the neck and pushed me out the door, yelling, "Read the sign, boy! Is this any place for you to beg for food?" Looking up, I saw the shop-window sign: "State-Owned Cafeteria." With me there, that establishment wouldn't have reflected very well on the state.

I stopped at the cafeteria again in 1996 on my way to see my family in northern Shaanxi. By then it was a privately owned restaurant.

Upon leaving the cafeteria I noticed a military vehicle with a trailer full of coal. A man with insignia on his collar and cap was stepping out of the vehicle. I had learned as a child how wonderful the People's Liberation Army was. So I walked up to him, knelt before him and sobbed, "Officer, sir, I'm starving to death. Could you please find it in your heart to give me a little something to eat?" But he ignored me. I looked up and realized he was staring at some attractive women passing by. He had heard nothing of what I said. My begging failed again and I had no food.

I endured the hunger and walked to the town bus station. My brain was still functioning well—I knew I should go to the station and follow the direction the buses were headed so that I wouldn't lose my way home. By then I had given up the idea of begging for food. I lay down at the bus station entrance, with my stomach rumbling from hunger. The freezing weather made my body quiver, but I lay there for a while.

Late in the evening I heard a voice say, "What happened to you, child? Why are you sleeping here?" I opened my eyes and replied to the older man who had bent down next to me: "I'm almost dead from starvation." He sighed and said, "Come with me."

The man, a stonemason, was around sixty years old. It was clear that he had just returned from work. He held a pipe in his mouth and had many cuts on his hands. As soon as we arrived at his place he quickly weighed two pounds of flour and made noodle soup out of it. He didn't even stop to wash his hands. I ate all of the noodles and broth. After eating we chatted for a little while, then I fell asleep in his bed. In the morning the man bought me a bus ticket to Yanan. He also gave me sixty-five cents to spend. Although I knew he earned only twenty cents a day, it didn't take me long to spend almost two dollars of his! I had very poor manners back then and left without even asking his name. I deeply regret acting that way.

The bus ride from Huangling to Yanan didn't seem to take long, although it covered more than sixty miles. I arrived in Yanan in the afternoon. I made a firm decision to buy something to eat, so I spent one cent on a snack called "sheep's skin" and bought seven dumplings for another two cents. I spent three cents in total.

I thought of how no one in my family had eaten dumplings for a long time, even since before my father had passed away. That night, as I had done before, I slept at the bus station entrance. I woke up before sunrise when I heard the bus engines start up. Then I began to walk in the direction of my hometown.

The sun rose after I had walked a little over six miles. I saw an old Liberation Army vehicle. The driver stood on the vehicle's bumper, doing repair work. Beside the car was a bucket. I immediately picked up the bucket and went off to find water for him, even though I wasn't quite sure whether the radiator needed water. Having eventually found water in a trench more than a third of a mile away, I got a little worried… did the driver really need a bucket of water? Would he be able to give me a lift?

When I returned, without even looking at me the driver snatched the bucket, poured the water into the receptacle and handed back the bucket. I was so glad and went to fetch another bucket of water. After he poured the second bucket of water in, the vehicle started. Without even asking me where I wanted to go he said, "Let's go." I went to sit beside him in the front seat but he quickly said, "Not here! Go to the back." As I think back, I realize he must have said that because I was filthy and smelled bad.

That was a terrific trip. Yanan is at least one hundred seventy miles from Suide. We arrived there that evening. Although Suide was another sixty miles from my hometown, I felt very close to accomplishing my mission.

That night, while it was still very dark, I felt someone kick me in the bottom and then heard someone yell at me, "Hey, thief! What are you doing? This is the people's militia talking."

"Have you seen me do anything?" I asked.

"Don't you dare talk back! Let's go!"

The militia group took me to a guardroom. An old man there was burning charcoal in a metal drum to warm himself. The militia group handed me over to the man and told me, "We'll be back tomorrow to deal with you!" They then went out to patrol.

I cried and explained to the old man what I had been through. I thought that after explaining myself, my story of misery might move him and he would let me go. He listened to me for a while, then stood up and went out, locking the door behind him without saying a word. I thought perhaps he felt I was complaining too much. However, he came back shortly, took two sweet potatoes out of his pockets and put them on the charcoal fire. When they were cooked, he put the sweet potatoes into my hands. Finally he spoke to me and said, "Eat them, child! I know you are not a bad person. They want to send you to the quarry tomorrow to collect stones. It would be for an indefinite duration, depending on when they wanted to release you. You have to leave here quickly. Become a soldier and find your way to success. The worst possible consequence of my letting you go is that they beat me tomorrow."

Although begging for food in Huangling county was hard, I came across many good people throughout my journey.

After arriving home, I couldn't help crying upon seeing my family again. It had been so long. For the last few years the family had been separated, each going his or her own way to find enough to eat. Whenever any of us saw each other, we would always cry before we could talk. It was hard to leave each other, and even harder to meet again.

My mother did not approve of the idea of my enlisting in the military. She reminded me that during my father's illness my older brother and sister had donated much of their blood for him because we didn't have enough money to help him in any other way. My brother, in particular, had given so much blood that his health eventually collapsed. After my father passed away, all of the family's burdens had fallen on this same brother's shoulders. My mother was worried about him and didn't want me to enlist.

"I've made up my mind all the same!" I shouted at my weeping mother. "Since you can't manage to have me go to school, you can't manage my life. I have to make my own decisions." Finally, my mother no longer insisted and gave up. I feel very sorry for having said that back then.

My three years of military service had a big impact on my life. First of all, I came to know the outside world, a world very different from my home and from the lives of civilian working people. I also came to see things from different perspectives, or, I should say, I came to see the processes and circumstances surrounding things in a different way. My hopes and dreams also changed and grew: I went from hoping I would have enough to eat to hoping the army could arrange for a job for me. At that time, however, everyone knew about the standard bias against people from rural areas; soldiers from there were always sent back to where they came from, jobless.

In the end, just like the others, I received demobilization orders, which meant I had to go back home and resume life as a peasant. When I heard the news I was standing up, but immediately fell to my knees, and my nose began to bleed. One never knows how the body might react when one's dreams are dashed.

Perseverance Rewarded by Heaven

After I was demobilized from the army, I had several part-time jobs doing all kinds of things. I sold vegetables out of a small cart on the street and did basically any work I could find. I was in a very awkward and trying situation. But I had hope that things would turn around.

Back when I was selling vegetables in 1991 there weren't any plastic bags available, so many of the vendors used newspapers to wrap the vegetables. I remember well the day when I sold a vegetable to someone, and he used half a piece of newspaper to wrap it and left the other half on the ground. As I picked up the other half I saw that it was the *Legal Daily News*. The paper said that over the next ten years China would need 150,000 lawyers, and that the best way to obtain lawyer qualifications was to first complete a vocational degree in law through self-study. After reading the report I was eager to give it a try. I told myself that, at worst, even if I passed only one subject a year, then it would take me just fourteen years to pass all of them.

During the next few years I studied every moment I could, even while walking. When riding the bus, one of my hands would hold the handrail and the other would hold a textbook. I would always remind myself that I was using my energy constructively and moving toward success. As a result, I was fortunate enough to pass all three subjects I had enrolled in the first semester. Within two and a half years I passed all fourteen subjects and in 1994 earned my diploma in law.

All of us were jubilant on graduation day, and many of us celebrated with friends and family. I wasn't overly excited, though, as earning a diploma wasn't my ultimate goal; I knew that if I was to become licensed to practice I would need to pass the bar exam.

After being given my diploma I went straight to a bookstore. I skimmed the books necessary to prepare for the exam and by the time I finished I was perspiring all over. The passage rate at the time was only one percent! The successful examinees were all from prestigious universities, but I was an independent student and almost thirty years old. So the passage rate for someone like me was basically zero.

I paced back and forth in the bookstore for a long while. I couldn't decide whether to buy the books, which cost twenty-four dollars. My family was still living in poverty then, and twenty-four dollars was no small amount. And then there was the likelihood of failure... After putting considerable thought into it I decided to buy the books.

Passing the bar exam was an arduous task. It brought to mind the ancient story of Yu the Great, who was so determined to find a long-term solution to the flooding problem that he didn't see his family for years, even when he walked right past their door.

My level of determination was similar.

To facilitate our studies three months prior to the exam, four other students and I rented a room together for twenty-six cents per night. I would study through the night and stop at 5:00 A.M.; afterwards I would splash cold water on my face and hurry off to work. I was full of energy. I felt that if only one person passed the exam, that person would be me. "I'll surely be a lawyer someday!" I told myself. My energy gave me the strength to endure those difficult times and to pass the exam that year.

What a dramatic time in life. Every year before the exam, the Lawyers Association asks a veteran attorney to lecture to the students preparing for it. There were five hundred students at the lecture I attended in 1994. Young adults, of course, like to compare themselves to each other. So a lot of people looked down on examinees of my poor educational background. One day when everyone was relaxing during a break from lecture I said, "You wouldn't be feeling so proud of yourselves right now if I told you a statistic. If we examinees here in Xinjiang province follow the national average, only five out of the five hundred of us are going pass the exam this year."

An arrogant military officer in his early twenties quipped, "Gao Zhisheng, even if one hundred of us pass the exam, you won't be one of them!"

In those days I had a very fragile ego, and I was also overly image conscious. So I immediately went up to him and grabbed him by the collar, sneering, "What's your name?"

He replied, "I am Fang Xiaopo," which wasn't true. "Do you want to fight me?"

I said with a roar, "Fang Xiaopo, you will be here next year, listening to me lecture!"

While the officer was still in shock I added, "Remember the name Gao Zhisheng. It will stay with you for the rest of your life!"

In an equally confident tone the officer replied, "Fine! Everybody here is a witness: He doesn't have to be a lecturer here next year—if he simply passes the exam, I'll call him 'teacher' for the rest of my life!"

The following year, as I thought, I stood at the podium of the lecture hall and addressed the examinees. Fang Xiaopo was one of them.

As I walked up to the podium I called out "Fang Xiaopo!"

In line with his military way he replied "present" and immediately stood at attention.

I said, "Take a seat. Last year we agreed to study together this year, in this very classroom. It looks like we both kept our promise. The only difference is, this year you are facing me."

From then on we were good friends.

I had a good lecture that day. After the lecture Fang came up to me and asked, "Mr. Gao, how did you manage to get to this position in just one try?" I said, "My young friend, you won't even manage to pass the exam this year. How could you possibly understand what it took for me to get here?"

I was being honest with him. It really wasn't as simple as "in just one try."

That year I often got up early and practiced lecturing to a wheat field. The stalks were my examinees.

Whenever I had the time I would go out to try to establish myself. Winter in Urumqi was very cold—so cold that when I went out my facial muscles would nearly freeze. I was still very poor then and wore only thin clothes, so when I arrived at an office building where I needed to do business, I would always go straight to the restrooms, as they had heaters. I would stay there until my facial muscles relaxed enough for me to be able to speak freely. Then I would go to the particular person's office.

Most lawyers in China establish themselves by boasting of their connections with judges. I didn't have such connections and would just speak plainly. I gave forty-seven free lectures on the legal system to universities, factories, enterprises, and military troops. The largest audience I gave a lecture to consisted of a few thousand. Most of the places at which I gave lectures became my clients later on.

I used a similar approach to gain the opportunity to teach the examinees. In preparation for approaching the Lawyers Association, I designed and printed teacher evaluation forms to obtain feedback on my lectures. I took the forms with me and went to talk with the authorities at the Association, telling them that I wanted to give lectures to examinees. They were quite surprised and asked me who I was. I told them, "I was one of last year's examinees, so I know best what the examinees need. If you give me a chance this year, and if even five out of the five hundred people I lecture to think my lecture isn't good, then afterwards I'll stand at the door and let each examinee slap me in the face."

None of what I did to earn the privilege of giving lectures to the examinees was to prove myself to Fang Xiaopo or the others. Rather, I did it because I was passionate about the challenge of preparing future lawyers for the profession.

I never accepted any money as a gift from any organization, and never accepted invitations to be treated to meals. Whenever I gave a lecture I would refuse at least sixty-five to eighty dollars of extra gift money. I always took the bus home and would get off one or two stops early to save even one cent. Because I couldn't afford to eat out I was often hungry. My purpose that year was to train myself thoroughly in public speaking, use of legal terminology, and handling of a large audience. It was a tempering process and a test of endurance, all of which helped me build a strong lawyer's ethic.

II. Returning to the Cave

Returning to the place where Mother gave birth to me and raised me, wherever my eyes wander, from this cave dwelling to the courtyard or the mountain road, memories are everywhere. My mother's image, voice, and smiling face are everywhere in my mind.

Lunar New Year

Written on lunar New Year's Day, January 2006, at Mother's north Shaanxi cave dwelling

The lunar New Year celebration has special significance in the countryside. It is the greatest and most important holiday for rural Chinese communities.

This is because unlike any other time of the year, during the Spring Festival[3] people from the countryside have the opportunity to eat a good meal and put on some nice clothes. Families who get together only once a year reunite for this period of time. Children from relatively wealthy families are given New Year's money, firecrackers, and so on.

The most memorable New Year's celebration I can recall is the first one after my father passed away. I'll never forget the excitement of counting down the days to New Year's. My brothers and I were so eager for firecrackers, something I can barely understand now. That first New Year's after Dad's death, we cried because we couldn't have any firecrackers. And in fact, we didn't play with the other children our age during that season because we didn't have firecrackers. Another reason we stayed away, though, was because our family couldn't afford new clothes as the other children's families could. But we did often sneak away to catch a glimpse of the other children playing in their new clothes. We were all thinking the same thing: It would be a relief if some of them, or even just one, didn't have any new clothes, like us. Somehow that never happened.

Half a year after Dad passed away New Year's came, and we had to face the idea of celebrating without a father. It was the first time we dreaded all the festivities. As the New Year approached, our entire household was engulfed in sadness. I was just over ten years old, yet even I felt sullen. I can still remember that four days before New Year's we had not yet spent even a cent in preparation. The reality was, we didn't have even a cent to spare for New Year's goods, and neither did we own anything with which to celebrate. Mother was still beside herself with grief over Dad's death, and she didn't bother even trying to conceal her low spirits. On the twenty-seventh day of the last month in the lunar calendar, my mother, eyes red and puffy from crying, asked me

3 Another name for the Chinese lunar New Year.

to go with her on a short trip. Nobody in the family was bold enough to ask where she was going. With a quick glance at my older brothers, I left holding my mother's hand.

We walked in silence for three hours before arriving at a village called Xishan, which was over six miles from home. That was the furthest from home that I had ever been. My mother told me that she had a blind paternal aunt who lived in the village. We went to her house, but as it turned out, Mother's aunt and her adopted son were just as poor as we were. After drinking some gruel with them, we prepared to leave. Mother's aunt began to cry as she stroked my mother's head and face, and tears flowed from her blind eyes. A little later she hobbled over to another room and scooped out a bowlful of yellow bean sprouts. She wrapped them up and gave them to my mother.

On the way back, we walked especially slowly and I could sense that my mother was pondering something. After walking about half way it grew dark. When we arrived at a brook about a mile and a quarter from home, she sat down on a rock and began sobbing like a child. As I held my mother's hand I could feel her shaking. Her hand was damp with sweat.

After quite a long time she stopped crying and wiped her face with her clothes. Then she stroked my head twice and wiped my tears away with her hand. She said in a trembling voice, "Oh Guan Yin, Goddess of Mercy, please bless these pitiable fatherless children! …Runhui (my nickname), your dad has gone. Mother is at a loss, but don't worry, I won't always be like this. After the New Year I'll be fine." When Mom and I got home, the family was anxiously waiting for us.

When God closes a door, somewhere he opens a window. On New Year's Eve four days later, we had more than a pound of pork—a gift from my father's brother. Then on New Year's Day we ate dumplings stuffed with radish and mixed with that meat.

Starting that New Year's, my mother's resoluteness and tenaciousness came back. Her long-lasting sorrow was overcome by her love and feeling of responsibility for us. My mother became a strong person again, and passed on that strength to us.

An Old Copper Ladle

Written January 26, 2006, at Mother's cave dwelling

After we lost our father in 1975, we didn't even have anything to sell to survive. We were a poor family before my father died, but after borrowing so much money from others we became even poorer. My mother didn't know what to do with herself and her seven children.

I remember that when we used to wake up in the morning, my mother's bed was always empty. Working hard from dawn to dusk was the only way she knew for our family to survive. We used to wait for her to return home after it was already very dark. The memory of my mother sitting on the doorstep to rest for a while after work every day is still vivid. She was always silent at those times. We understood that it was because she was exhausted from work. After a while she would get up slowly and bring her tired body inside to cook dinner.

The first year after Dad died, Mom wept often because he was gone and we had nothing. Tears would stream down when she was cooking, eating, working, and at any moment. Every time she wept, we couldn't help but weep with her. The neighbors would come and try to comfort us. Although I was very little then, I was pained every time I saw my mother's sadness.

One summer afternoon I accompanied my mother to a well to fetch water. Our village's well was halfway up a mountain. There was a narrow path—only one person wide—leading to the well. When people went to get water they would carry copper ladles with them to fill their buckets. By noontime the sun was so hot it had become utterly silent in the mountains. After my mother had filled the bucket she went to place the ladle back on the hook hanging over the side of the bucket, but missed. Suddenly the ladle fell down into the well—a seventy-degree slope lined with lots of little stones. As the ladle rolled down over the stony slope it hit the stones with a clang. It was an old copper ladle. None of us knew how old it was or who had used it before our family. My mother stood there stupefied and began to cry, looking at the copper ladle despairingly as it swiftly rolled away. My older brother was laboring nearby and thought that my mother had hurt herself. He shouted and ran toward my mother. She said to him "Liyi," which was his nickname, "What can I do now? I've lost the ladle in the well!"

The old copper ladle was worth less than twenty-five cents. People nowadays may think that losing such a ladle is nothing and that we were overly concerned, but for a family like ours, it was a major misfortune. We had heavy hearts for several hours, until my mother somehow managed to retrieve it from the well with strenuous effort.

Now, over twenty years later, I can still hear the clang of the copper ladle falling into the well, and my mother's despairing cry.

A Handful of Fried Soybeans

Written January 26, 2006, at Mother's cave dwelling

Mother gave away this cave dwelling, where I was born, to some other people several years ago. We children were all born and raised in this cave. The brick bed in the cave is plenty large when only four people lie down on it, but it becomes a bit crowded if five people lie on it. When my father was alive, all nine of us would sleep on it. One of my brothers, my father, and I all slept under the same blanket until my father passed away. No one in the family was able to have a blanket all to himself. I remember that every evening when we were going to sleep my parents would arrange us, working to meet our needs. Later in life my mother would often say, jokingly, "Getting you all comfortable in bed at night would always leave me in a sweat!" Mom certainly raised us under tough conditions.

Just beyond the yard outside, there is a trail leading off to civilization. During the three years when I was in middle school, my mother would invariably gaze off after me as I walked to school every day on the trail. In the evening she would again be there, standing at the end of the trail waiting for me. Whether on the coldest days of winter or the hottest days of summer, rain, hail or shine, she would always be there. Every time she heard my footsteps as I ran down the mountain trail she would shout my childhood nickname. After hearing my response she would usually hurry inside to heat some food for me.

One evening when I came back from school she was standing on the trail waiting for me as usual, but this time she didn't go inside on hearing my response. I walked up to her and sensed that something was wrong. She cupped my face in her hands and said, "Runhui, listen to your mother, we have no food left now. I went with your brother to visit our relatives in Xiawa village today to borrow some, but they couldn't give us any. I can't give you anything to eat tonight, but tomorrow I will definitely have something. Go to sleep a little early tonight." She then took my hand and we went inside. That night, I wept softly for quite some time. Most of the pillow became wet with my tears. It wasn't because I was hungry, as I understood the position my mother was in after my father died so young. I was thinking of the great burden on my mother simply to keep us alive, and now there was nothing to feed us that night. Where could we find food? That night I heard Mom tossing and turning. She couldn't fall asleep for a long time.

Before dawn the next morning, Mom woke me up to get ready for school as usual. Upon seeing me off she gave me a handful of fried soybeans. They were somewhat moist. Judging by their temperature, I knew they had been held tightly in her hand for a while. Because the sky was still very dark I couldn't see my mother's face. But tears rolled down mine like a broken strand of beads. I insisted that she give me only some of the beans so that she could give the rest to my equally hungry younger brothers and sisters. She wouldn't agree. I did not leave for school but cried loudly and kept insisting. Mom stayed calm, but gave me a firm shove onto the trail to school.

That day when I returned in the evening, my mother was standing on the trail. After shouting my name, she hurried inside. I knew she had borrowed some food for our survival.

Twenty-eight years have passed, yet this scene has never faded from my memory.

My Common-Folk Mother

Written March 11, 2005, beside Mother's coffin

My mother left the world she loved at 4:24 P.M. on March 6, 2005. It is the end of an era for the seven of us brothers and sisters, who are to go on without parents.

Her condition worsened just as I arrived in Beijing for a case involving a group of elderly people, similar in age to my mother, who had been pleading their case to the authorities for ten years.

I received a phone call from my brother, and an ominous feeling came over me. My forty-year-old brother was sobbing on the other end of the line. I panicked. My world went blank and filled itself with enormous pain and sorrow. The next thing I knew I was on the floor of a hospital, weeping, aware only of the coldness of the floor beneath my face. By the time my wife and mother-in-law helped me up, most of my face felt numb. My vision became blurry from the lack of oxygen to my brain. I cried the whole way home from the hospital. Then I prepared to drive back to my hometown through the night. When evening came, I was on my way, with a thousand miles ahead of me and a feeling of emptiness and loss.

What is usually a five–hour drive took me eight hours, as my mind was in a daze. The trip felt extraordinarily long. I stopped for an hour at my sister's place in Taiyuan, and then she and I continued the sorrowful journey.

This is the first time that my mother wasn't here to welcome me back to our little mountain village, a place that is still poor but remains dear to my heart. My mother will never be here again… The whole family has been wailing in mourning for her.

At first sight of my mother's sealed coffin I couldn't contain my emotions. I knelt down and crawled toward it. I was once again overwhelmed by the loss...

Father's Unfulfilled Wish Becomes Mother's Aspiration

Our sixty-seven-year-old mother has left us forever. She lived sixty of her sixty-seven years in poverty and hardship.

My mother lost her father when she was only six years old and became a child bride when she was eight. She often told us about her misery during those years as a child bride. Although she was a child bride for only four years (she escaped and ran back to her mother's home at the age of twelve), she had suffered so much that even to the end of her life, she had not been able to tell all her sad stories.

When she was fifteen she moved with her mother to a small mountain village where she lived for the remaining fifty-two years of her life. The village had a scant population of just over two hundred people when she passed away. You can imagine what a small place it is.

My mother married my father when she was sixteen. According to my aunt, my father's family was very poor at the time, and my mother and father continued to live in poverty for the remaining twenty-two years of their marriage. The only thing that didn't change during those twenty-two years was the poverty. My aunt told us that although they had very little throughout their marriage, and even until my father's death, my mother and father had always been happy together. The oldest child in the family was born when Mom was seventeen. My grandmother died at age forty-one when Mom was twenty-five and I was a newborn of only forty days. I remember how she often grew teary-eyed when she talked about our grandmother. Her feelings for Grandma touched people.

My father died of cancer at the age of forty-one. The sadness that engulfed my mother and our family over the loss of my father is beyond description.

My father had a life-long wish that one day there would be enough food for the family. However, he passed away with the wish unfulfilled. So my mother took up his wish and aspired to one day have enough for the whole family. Things were unusually hard for all of us when Dad was sick, and this burdened Mom greatly. We sold whatever we could to pay for his treatments. And we children donated so much blood for him that there wasn't enough left in our own bodies—my oldest brother couldn't walk properly because of it. But he was the only one old enough to earn money, doing manual labor.

When my father's body was laid out on the floor of our home, we were not only weighed down by loss, but had the additional burden of debts owed to the hospital. The whole family, especially Mom, felt helpless in the face of the debt, just as we did at the loss of our father. We didn't have the money to buy him a coffin and bury him so that he could be laid to rest. As she stared at my deceased father lying on the floor, my poor mother wailed in pain and despair. Part of it was that we had nothing to eat, and we children were starving. And the only one old enough to work—my oldest brother—barely had the strength to carry himself upright after having donated so much blood and having nothing nutritious to eat for recovery. Mom and we children felt that we were at a dead end.

There is a line in an ancient poem that reads, "As [the weary traveler] despairs over finding no road, a village appears and the shade of willows and bright flowers beckons." My mother didn't have such fortune, however. For the next twenty years she always struggled under straitened circumstances.

On June 22, 1975, thanks to the help of many people, we obtained a coffin for my father, which cost a little over five dollars. My father was tall, so his body had to be bent to fit into the coffin. It was, in a sense, a reminder of how he lived—never able to stand straight, always weighed down by life's burdens.

After we finally "succeeded" in burying him, we began a ten-year battle for survival. My mother was our commander in battle and our moral support. She bore the greatest burden and took on the greatest tasks in the exhausting endeavor.

She worked day and night to support us. During the day she worked in the fields. People could often hear her crying while she worked, and they sometimes shed empathetic tears. When she returned home at dusk, just cooking dinner was enough to exhaust her. All the same she had to continue working even after we children went to bed. She would spin cotton yarn under the dim kerosene lamp and would sometimes work through the night. This was the only way she could ensure that all her children would have clothes to wear. Sometimes I would wake up during the night, and each time would hear the sound of the spinning wheel, often accompanied by weeping.

My mother lost a lot of weight and became very thin in less than six months after my father's death. Her hard work, however, was still not enough to provide adequately for us. All of us children began to do whatever we could to help, in hopes that this might ensure our survival and reduce Mom's heavy burden. But misfortunes never come singly. On a dark night about a year after my father passed away, my oldest brother became extremely weak and ill, and lost consciousness. We carried him to the county hospital, and Mom was beside herself.

With one disaster after the next, the family was again and again thrown into desperate circumstances, but again and again, my mother, thin and slight of build, overcame them. Many kind people offered to introduce her to a man so that she could remarry and no longer have to bear such hardships, but she declined their well-intentioned offers. To those who tried to persuade her, she said firmly that she had resolved to successfully raise the children on her own, and that nothing would change her mind. She has indeed realized her goal.

Six Thousand Miles: Life as a Middle School Student

My mother had her eyes fixed on the future. Her breadth of vision had a great influence on us children and formed the foundation of our values today. My mother decided to send all of her children to school, except for our oldest brother and sister. Such an idea then seemed simply unachievable. However, all of us, beginning with our second oldest brother, completed middle school. Our education was essential in changing our fate for the better. Our second oldest brother had initially refused to go to school because he was worried about the burden it placed on my mother; however, my mother's decision was in no way negotiable. Even though our family was poor, my second oldest brother managed to finish high school, which helped him a lot—both when he joined the army and later in life. I finished my primary school education more or less through self-study, but our poverty wasn't the only reason I studied the way I did.

Starting the second year after Dad's death, my ten-year-old younger brother and I took up the responsibility of supporting the family for the first half of the year. This we did through our little medicinal herb business. Digging for the herbs in the mountains was grueling work, and we were so hungry that we didn't have the strength even to stand up straight. We would have a bowl of thin porridge at night before falling asleep on the floor.

At night my mother would begin the next step in the production process. She spent the whole night flattening the herbs with a rolling pin, pulling off the roots and rough fibers, and then arranging the herbs by category. This was to prepare them for drying in the sun the next day. The three of us worked together this way and used the herbs we sold at the market to buy red sorghum to eat. During the ten days between markets we were able to dig and dry over eleven pounds of medicinal herbs. At about fourteen cents per pound, we could bring in a little more than a dollar fifty each time. Sorghum in the husk was sold at about three cents a pound at the time. As soon as we had sold our herbs, the first thing we did was to buy forty-five pounds of sorghum for about a dollar thirty-five. This would be the food for the whole family for the next ten days. We would use the remaining money for other things, such as cooking salt and kerosene.

When autumn came and there were no more herbs to dig up, my mother instructed us to pick up the grain kernels that were left in the paddies and by the roadside after the agricultural cooperative had finished its autumn harvest. Usually we could find scattered kernels for two months, and this would help reduce by two months the period during which we had no source of food.

Winter on the Loess Plateau always brings harsh cold and strong wind. While other children stayed in their homes, daily we had to scavenge for firewood in the mountains due to lack of money to buy coal. The poverty and the adverse natural environment certainly tempered our will, with the help of our mother's unyielding spirit. This enabled us to survive over the years. I entered a new phase in life when in the latter part of 1977 Mother decided to send me to middle school. This phase lasted for three years.

As I sit next to Mom's coffin and think back to those three years in middle school I am pained inside at all that Mom put herself through for me. It was her stamina, industriousness, and sense of responsibility that enabled me to complete those years.

The Gucheng Middle School was located high in the mountains, about three miles away from home. It took me one and a half hours to walk there since I was still small then. As it would have cost an extra eight cents a day for food if I boarded at school, Mom encouraged me walk the distance and attend as a day student. Thus I started my three years of study, during which I walked a total of six thousand miles. My mother had not a single night of uninterrupted sleep during those years. I had to arrive at school each day by dawn. This required me to get up very early to get ready and then walk the one and a half hours. So I slept two and a half hours less each morning than I otherwise would have. But the sleep my mother sacrificed for my sake was much greater. No household in our village had a clock or a watch then. People still depended on the ancient way of telling time by observing the changes in the sky. As I slept, Mom would go out several times to look at the stars. On cloudy nights she didn't let herself sleep at all, as she had to judge the time by instinct.

Thanks to my mother's sacrifices and sense of responsibility I was never late once and never missed class for the entire three years. I made sure to live up to it by spending all my time on my studies. Reading and studying became my life's pattern. Even today, people still joke about the times when I did manual labor for them in exchange for novels and magazines to read. As far as grades are concerned, I was always among the top three students of the fifty or more in the class (my mischievousness was up there, too). After middle school, I passed the high school entrance exam and did well enough to attend one of the country's top high schools. Because we were poor, though, I unfortunately couldn't attend school anymore. My years of study in middle school had a significant impact on my life. They taught me study methods and laid the groundwork for self-study later in life. They made many things possible that would have otherwise been beyond reach. My mother and I achieved all of this through our combined efforts.

Mother's Moral Strength

My mother was a person of great moral strength. Yet her moral strength cannot be fully captured by the pen in my hand, nor even fully fathomed by my mind. It was something in her that deepened over the course of an entire lifetime.

Mom helped us understand through her own actions that there are consequences for every action, and that what is reaped is sown. She would punish us severely if we ate other people's gourds or fruit without permission, even though it was done out of hunger. Because of this trait of my mother's we learned from the time we were children never to pick up and pocket anything that belonged to someone else.

The filial piety my mother showed our grandma (my father's mother) was well-known in our area, far and wide. Oddly enough, we didn't have a very good impression of our grandma. As far as we could remember there were only three circumstances in which she didn't scold Mom: when she was eating, when she was sleeping, or when Mom was out. Mom often wept over it when Grandma wasn't around. She would tell us, though, that Grandma had a very hard life and remind us that Grandma had lost her husband when she was young and her son when she was old. Life was indeed very hard for her. Mom made clear to us that we were Grandma's only family, and that Grandma didn't have anyone else to let off steam with. If we understood how miserable Grandma was, she said, we would think nothing of her harshness.

Although my mother was often scolded to the point that tears ran down her face, as far as I recall, she always served my grandmother first at meals. When everyone else's food in the family was rationed during hard times, Grandma was the exception. When we had a large pot of thin rice porridge, Mom would scoop up thick porridge from the bottom to give to Grandma, who continued her scolding. The porridge left in the pot after that was thin. In the wintertime, our cave dwelling was so cold that the water jar we kept usually iced up by morning. Not so in Grandma's cave, which was heated and toasty warm. For this reason we all fought over who would get to sleep in Grandma's cave. Each market day, Mom would try to buy something nice for Grandma to eat. As I recall, this meant that we children were barred from Grandma's cave area for a few hours. Once the "ban" was lifted we would chatter about what sorts of treats we thought Mom had bought this time.

Although my mother lived sixty years of her life in hardship, she was constantly ready to lend a hand to other poor people, in any way she could. China has always had a large number of impoverished people, but that was even more the case in those years. The people who begged were poor, and those who didn't were also poor.

My mother was known for her hospitality toward poor people, even though she lived in poverty herself. In winter, no matter where a beggar came from, nor how many of them came, she invited them into our cave dwelling. During the day she provided them with a place to relax; at night she provided them with a place to sleep. Sometimes the cave would hold as many as ten of them. Winter nights on the Loess Plateau are extremely cold, and the cold there combined with strong wind can chill to the bone. Although our humble cave dwelling wasn't very warm, it did provide sufficient shelter from the bitter cold and wind. People in need stayed with us for every winter I can remember; so many passed through that even our mother lost track. Whenever people in need came to our village, the residents would tell them to go see my mother.

Since becoming an attorney twenty years later, I have often received in my office persons—particularly from the disadvantaged population—sent to me by warmhearted colleagues. Some of them have used canes to walk, and some have been confined to wheelchairs. They are people who can't afford to pay legal fees. Whenever this has happened, scenes of my mother welcoming such people into her home have come to mind, bringing a smile to my face. As I recall those scenes today I find myself weeping. My mother is gone now and lies in the coffin in front of me.

Two memories of my mother's good deeds remain particularly fresh in my mind. On a terribly windy night in the dead of winter, Mom learned that a group of poor people who had been outside begging had found their way into an abandoned cave dwelling. Although my mother had already gone to bed upon learning the news, she got right up and took us to look for those poor souls. I remember vividly what happened. When we arrived at the cave where they were, we saw that they had covered the entrance with a pile of straw. Moving the straw aside uncovered a heart-breaking scene: eight people huddled together in the cold, male and female, old and young.

My mother then told them why we had come. They had evidently been startled by us so didn't respond. They looked at us, and then at each other. In the end, they believed what my mother said. That night a large group of needy people (which included us) crowded into our home. There were people everywhere—on the bed, on the floor.

The other memory is from a summer day. A woman beggar with a child came to our place. As it happened, though, we ourselves had nothing to eat at that time and were in no position to offer her anything. The woman was quite disappointed. She took her child's hand and began to leave. My mother then told her to wait for a moment. Soon my mother came back with two corn cobs that weren't quite ripe. It turned out that our mother had gone to the family plot and broken off the cobs for the woman.

My mother believed that one is rewarded for acts of kindness, so she did good deeds throughout her life. Her reverent faith in Buddha often moved people.

With the first year of my law practice my mother's life changed for the better and she was soon out of poverty. By then, all her children had grown up and were successful in their own lives, so her main focus had become to pay reverence to Buddha and do good works. I gave her material support in every way I could, and was often touched by her faith in Buddha and willingness to help others. One example of her generosity was her efforts to help those whose graves had been robbed. A few years ago this was on the rise, and the remains from these graves were scattered about. My mother spared no effort and used her own money to buy wooden boxes so that the remains could be buried properly. At festivals, she had her grandchildren burn paper money as an offering to those people's spirits.

Once out of poverty my mother never forgot the poor. Each time we went home to celebrate the lunar New Year in recent years, we would see other people and their children at our home who had come to eat with us. They were in shabby clothes, and we had no idea who they were. When we asked Mom, she would always say with a knowing smile, "They're our relatives."

One day during this year's Spring Festival a thin man with two children came to our home. Mom was sick at the time. When she saw them she said to us with difficulty, "This is your cousin." She then told my sister and sister-in-law to cook for them and treat them well (by that point we had all just finished our meal and cleaned up everything). She emphasized that we must make sure that both the adult and the children ate their fill. Upon hearing both of the children coughing constantly she asked my sister and me to give them money so that they could go to see a doctor.

Sometime afterward my brother told me that those had been beggars from a neighboring village, and that my mother had adopted them as relatives. He said that they often came to my mother's place to eat during holidays. Grinning, he added, "Mom has a lot of these sorts of relatives."

We have virtually adopted two poor children from our village since their father died, and I've been helping them regularly with their school fees. They always spend holidays with us, and we are truly like family. In preparing for our mother's funeral they fulfilled their filial duties just as if they were her own children. This touched us, and made us realize all the more the greatness of the mother we had lost.

My mother gave her heart and soul to us seven children. Even on her deathbed she kept repeating the names of all her children and grandchildren. She repeated our names again and again, and just kept doing so until she breathed her last. Whenever I think of this, the pain I feel is beyond description. The degree of love and care my mother showed us over the last few months of her life was deeply moving to all of us.

While it's true that every child probably feels his or her mother is the best, my feelings about my mother are as deeply felt as they come. I am not saying this simply because I'm writing an essay about her. My mother was a woman of indomitable spirit. I say this with full confidence each time it is uttered. My mother was one of the common folk, but this has no bearing on her greatness of character, which was borne out in the very details of her daily life. She spent a great deal of her life in adverse circumstances, and yet never stopped offering a hand to those who were equally needy. Tears fell as I wrote about my mother helping others when she herself was in poverty. She displayed tremendous generosity and charity, in the broadest sense of the word. Her great character has had an impact on us throughout our lives, and it will do so into the future. Though poor most of her life, Mom gave us an abundance of riches. Over the last few days, the family has been sharing memories of Mom's great character in tears. We share the feeling that even if we were to die the cruelest of deaths, it would in no way compensate for the sacrifice and effort that she put in for us.

My mother is worthy of a book, yet she couldn't read a single word. Remembering my mother gives me a somber joy. It would be impossible to record all the memories of her greatness in an essay, or even in one hundred essays. I nevertheless had to write something to express how deeply I miss my great, beloved mother.

Before I finish, I have decided to drive alone to the village called Wangjiachuan and find the cave dwelling in which my mother was born...

Her spirit will live in our hearts always.

We have lost our mother, and have lost her forever. This stark truth will be with us for the rest of our lives.

Mom, with her slight build, bore all the trials and tribulations of life with remarkable fortitude, yet we children almost cannot bear the pain of losing her.

二

A Lonely Mission

The Plight of China's Lawyers

The first case I handled when I became an attorney was pro bono. Ever since then, for several years now, one third of my energy has been spent on providing free legal aid to indigent clients. After moving to Beijing, once I had earned enough money to no longer worry about having enough clothes to stay warm or enough food to eat, I put more energy into the bigger and farther-reaching domains—injustice done to specific groups and injustice in the social system as a whole.

The first concern for an attorney when handling a case is undoubtedly to ensure the litigant's lawful rights and interests. But with every case I hope that it will also enable more people to appreciate the importance of society's development and fairness. It can then be said that we have gone beyond the mere gains of an individual case.

For example, when giving legal assistance to a child victim of medical malpractice, it is important to consider not only the fate of the injured child, but also larger issues of social justice and the impact of the legal intricacies on the system. Or, when taking a case involving the sale of a state-owned enterprise, one can't let a wrong judicial decision impede the privatization of state industries, for that would impede industrialization and the completion of China's economic reform.

As to the government's intrusion into and forcible demolition of private homes, although there has been a law in the constitution since 1954 protecting private ownership of housing, in as early as 1956, the socialist reform fatally damaged the protection of private property and its owners. The damage continues to this day, in the 21st century.

Apart from working on legal cases, in recent years I have also published some articles, so I'm known for this in certain social spheres. Last year, for example, I wrote several articles denouncing the forced demolition of citizens' private property. My purpose was to, at a minimum, correct the insulting label of so-called "nail households,"[1] as the state-run media terms them. Exactly because of these articles, over the past two years the domestic media has been finding ways to restrict my speech.

Today the representative of a government agency said to me, "Shedding the blood of citizens is not what the central authorities desire." I replied, "Right, I don't think the central authorities would order officials at every level to treat citizens cruelly. But the central authorities aren't keeping such behavior under control, aren't dealing with it, and may be deliberately turning a blind eye to it. Yet the central authorities are responsible for it."

They explained to me that the government had issued repeated injunctions to stop the local authorities from injuring citizens. I said, "What are 'repeated injunctions'? Are they above or beneath the consti-

1 In that they stick out, as might a nail, by refusing to submit to state authority. The term suggests stubbornness or peskiness.

tution? If even our great national constitution is considered meaningless, how could repeated injunctions be effective?"

They went on to say that the Chinese people are inept, and that if they were allowed to demonstrate, society would surely break out into chaos. I asked them, "Then why do you have 'freedom of assembly and demonstration' inscribed in the constitution? Is it to deceive the common people, or to set a trap for them? You could just go ahead and remove these rights from the constitution. Although it would be shameless to do so, at least then the shamelessness would be on paper. What would be on paper would be shameless, and it would show that the constitution is for real, not for pretense."

China's dark side is so very, very large, especially when it comes to the system harming the citizens. That is far from all of it, though. A sad fact is that everywhere throughout the country, when you communicate with staff on official and even unofficial occasions, you find—to your surprise—that they fully approve of what the government does. This alone suggests the powerlessness of one individual to change things. It also says something of the incredible capacity of the state propaganda machine to brainwash the citizenry.

Take, for instance, the 1989 Tiananmen demonstration. This was a situation that could have been solved through non-violent means, yet the government chose to use bullets and tanks. Afterwards, people thought that the government had every right to open fire on and kill people, and that it did not need to admit to any mistake.

Beijing resident Ye Guozhu and three generations of his family lost all of their houses and property due to forced relocation. Applying for a permit to hold a protest against this, however, led to his being sentenced to prison for "disturbing social order." This was another case where people accepted what the government did without a second thought. Many of them said, "The government's demolition was right and lawful, and Ye Guozhu's request to keep his family's housing was unreasonable."

When I've told state-employed personnel about my dealings with Falun Gong[2] adherents, the question—throughout China—has almost always been the same: "When you look into their eyes, how glazed over are they?" They didn't ask whether the Falun Gong believers' eyes seemed glazed over. Rather, they just asked, "How glazed over were they?" They are convinced that the Falun Gong aren't normal people. The problem is that this impression they have is not something acquired through actual dealings with Falun Gong practitioners, but has been successfully instilled in them through the state propaganda machine.

I remember well the excitement that came with becoming a lawyer. I thought that the government was bound to support me in my quest to uphold justice. After some time, however, I grew hopelessly pessimistic. My dream of improving society had turned into a nightmare. Over the past few years I have become more coolheaded and realistic, and made huge adjustments to the way I do things. For example, every day three or four groups of people come to my office seeking my help in ensuring the protection of their rights and interests. Many people think it's pointless for me to meet with them, and I'm certainly not foolish enough to think their cases are likely to go anywhere. However, full of despair and anger these people come to Beijing to file petitions.[3] That's the condition they are in when they come to see me. When they phone me I don't have the heart to refuse them. Every time I meet with such people, I tell them, "I may not be able to provide a substantial solution

2 A spiritual discipline involving tai-chi like exercises and moral teachings whose adherents are persecuted by China's regime.

3 China is host to a longstanding cultural and legal tradition known as "petitioning," whereby any citizen can file a complaint with authorities, seeking the redress of grievances or abuses not satisfactorily addressed via other channels. Many Chinese travel great distances to petition in provincial capitals or Beijing, where established "petitions offices" exist.

to your problem, but I am willing to listen to your painful experience and to discuss with you how we might solve the problem, given the state of society today. That is all I can offer."

The regime does not see us lawyers as necessary, but legal assistance is urgently necessary for the many, many disadvantaged and downtrodden groups and individuals in society. This is the reality we lawyers face every day.

Our country operates without any regulations, or, put another way, regulations are routinely disregarded and abused. People's rights and interests are incessantly violated. Government officials are greedy and shameless, the law enforcement personnel break the law, an independent judiciary is non-existent, and society as a whole is dishonest and immoral… Having served as a lawyer these past seven years, I can say that we are immersed in this kind of atmosphere every day. Rule of law is a goal, but this goal requires a concrete system and procedures in place if it is to be realized. It also requires a genuine interest in pursuing it. In form, our society seems adequately civilized. In substance, however, the regime that rules it has never shed its thuggish ways. It says that the Party is all-powerful and that the administrative authority is far above the law, while in the same breath saying—no, shouting—that "this is a country ruled by law." To put it nicely, this is empty talk. To put it frankly, it's deception.

I had an idea for another very meaningful law that could be put in place—"Penal Code for Those of Disreputable Appearance"—under which anyone who isn't so nice to look at would be apprehended and severely punished. But then I thought about myself, and, a few glances in the mirror, plus constant jabs about my appearance from those around me, told me that the law wasn't a good idea. If it were enforced I might well be its first victim!

Behind Each Case, Systemic Problems

Things in China don't operate along the same lines as those in countries with an adequate legal system. The way that even very minor cases are handled here ultimately reflects covert, systemic problems. These problems are very real and extremely serious. You never know where you might be able to effect positive, systemic change. Simply wanting to make such changes, however, puts you in a very dangerous position.

Rules Governing Business Transactions Flouted

In November 2000 I moved from Xinjiang to Beijing. One of the reasons was because of a case related to the sale of a previously state-owned enterprise, filed against Xinjiang's Bazhou Prefecture.

The background of this case is that the Party's Fifteenth Political Consultative Conference proposed large-scale reform of state-owned enterprises, and when the local officials returned to the Bazhou area after the Conference, they aimed to demonstrate their compliance with the wishes of the Central Committee.[4] They therefore pushed through the sale of the Bazhou Farm Machinery Company, which was then the largest state-owned enterprise in the prefecture. This was their understanding of how to proceed in the spirit of the Conference.

The prefecture was economically depressed. Moreover, the Bazhou Farm Machinery Company was losing money every year, with annual losses totaling at least 13 million dollars. Naturally, no one wanted to buy it. One wonders, then, how the officials convinced anyone to do so. As it turns out, they set their sights on a man named Wu Anmin and told him, "You must buy this company. That is what China needs for its economic reform, development, and stability."

4 The Central Committee is a powerful body within the Party structure and consists of approximately three hundred members.

They subsequently actually "sold" the enterprise to that person. Two years later the enterprise started to turn a profit. So the politicians asked Mr. Wu to return the enterprise to the government. When asked why, they again said, "That is what China needs for its economic reform, development, and stability." Not a word more and not a word less.

The Bazhou officials called in the police and seized the enterprise under force. We then filed a lawsuit against the officials.

You know, Party officials at that level are not law conscious whatsoever, and, needless to say, don't understand the law. To our surprise, they phoned the director of the law firm that I was working for and ordered that our lawyers refrain from taking the case. I didn't know whether to laugh or cry at our firm's ridiculous response—they reached a "partnership agreement" with the officials that meant they would tell me to withdraw from the case. I told them that this was yet another indicator of our firm's spinelessness, and that I wasn't afraid to take the case. It turned out their decision was not based solely on fear, however. They explained, "Mr. Gao, you entered this profession less than two years ago. You don't understand the system. If you choose to keep doing things this way, you'll have to leave Xinjiang." So, just like that, I decided to come to Beijing.

The lawsuit lasted two years, with excellent results. Although my disloyal boss refused to pay me, everything turned out satisfactorily. The government returned the enterprise to Mr. Wu. In addition, because the government didn't have the money to pay the judgment, it deeded him land that was worth about 10 million dollars.

Cases Involving Demolished Homes Never Won

However many cases I have taken for citizens whom the government had forcibly "relocated" is the number I have lost. Unlike government statistics, this one is fully accurate. I have taken a case for each of seventy households in the Guangzhou University area. Yes, seventy households there were relocated.

Why, you may ask, is it impossible to successfully file and win a case against blatantly unlawful actions such as these? Because "relocations" are something that two of China's most powerful groups—real estate developers and their stooges, government officials at all levels—want. These entities are above the law. When they aren't bound by the law, how could one win a claim against them?

This past winter (in 2005), CCTV[5] aggressively promoted and broadcast the series called, "The Same Song." It spoke about the Guangzhou area, but instead of mentioning the area's many positive achievements, the expansion of the Guangzhou University campus was touted again and again, despite the huge number of homes that were turned to rubble by bulldozers and the many who were forced to relocate. I never watch CCTV, but I heard it in the background while my child was watching. I laughed as I listened. It reminded me of a similar incident several years ago when the media reported widely on the "positive value" of the Nanchizi district "revitalization" project in Beijing, in which nine hundred private homes were destroyed.

Many citizens nowadays share the following impression: whenever officials put a lot of effort into touting something among the public—whether via the media or other means—something shady is surely going on in the background. They can treat the laws they make as garbage, but they can never change the way that civilized societies view them.

The Special Case

Falun Gong cases are something I didn't touch until a few years ago, for one basic reason: Every attorney knows the government departments

5 China Central Television, China's main, state-run television broadcasting entity.

concerned do not allow lawyers to get involved. It's not necessary to find out whether anyone has seen any document decreeing this, nor to question whether the intent and resolve to block lawyers from taking these cases exists—it undoubtedly does. Ask any lawyer, and he will tell you that the prohibition was definitely put into place when Falun Gong was banned in 1999, although no lawyer has ever seen it in writing. The advantage of having an intangible decree is that, while constraining the lawyers, the authorities can, at any time, make a public statement that the "rumors" about this decree are "fabricated," thereby stifling any so-called "vicious attacks" on the Party and government.

When the new Hu-Wen[6] government was put in power, people had a range of opinions about what would happen. Some thought it would be different from the Jiang Zemin[7] era.

Many Falun Gong adherents and their family members have written letters to me since last July. The letters and also some visits heightened my awareness of the Falun Gong's plight. You could say that without looking into it, you won't know about it, but with only a little probing, you'll be shocked. At the end of 2004 I got involved in Huang Wei's case and, starting from the ground up, investigated everything I had heard over the years. Only then did I realize where the terror these people are experiencing was coming from—the entire "6-10 Office" system, which was controlling everything behind the scenes, and operating completely outside the law.

I normally have my assistant file lawsuits. Falun Gong was a special case, though, so I went to Shijiazhuang to work on Huang Wei's case with him. We took the case to three different courts. The response from two courts included three points: 1) Falun Gong cases are never allowed

---

6 That is, Hu Jintao and Wen Jiabao, China's number one and two political figures. Hu was made General Secretary of the Party in 2002, and Wen, Premier of the State Council in 2003.

7 Jiang served as General Secretary of the Party from 1989–2002, having been installed during the Tiananmen Massacre, and is thought to have masterminded the violent suppression of the Falun Gong.

to be filed; 2) no legal document would be written up, which meant we would not be allowed to follow the case up with any other court; 3) lawyers cannot be told what this decision is based on. The third court added one more point to these three, stating, "What you lawyers are doing is very risky. If you continue, we'll need to deal with you by writing a judicial report demanding disciplinary action against you."

How absurd that it has become "risky" for a lawyer to file a case against unlawful conduct based on the law! Simply for wanting to bring to justice the entity most responsible for the mess in this country and for the greatest violations of the law, I'm told the court needs to "deal with me"!

Today we are still fighting to be able to file Huang Wei's case. I sent the complaint to be filed via express mail to the courts, in hopes that they would be persuaded to act rationally and as civilized human beings who respect the citizens. I hoped that, with this understanding, we would be able to discuss the legal matters of the case. At the conclusion of a letter to the courts I added something like, "If you continue to be hostile toward China's legal values, continue to do things unlawfully, and therefore prevent the filing of this case, we will consider looking into it as a constitutional violation."

In addition, I published the "Open Letter to the National People's Congress,"[8] hoping that the involvement of top government officials might stomp out that horrendous behavior wherein citizens are unlawfully deprived of their constitutional rights and personal freedoms. Imagine… a lawyer having to go beyond laws and regulations simply to defend a litigant's legitimate rights and interests. That's anguish for a lawyer. There was no other way, so what else could be done?

---

8 A reference to Gao's first open letter regarding the suppression of Falun Gong. See chapter four.

Even today some of my friends still question why I took Huang Wei's case. Well, it would be a lie to say I never worry about my safety. For one, over the past year the relevant government departments have had countless "cordial" talks with me over the matter, in an attempt to dissuade me from continuing.

Being a lawyer I see it clearly and feel it deeply: The way China's authorities operate is not merely twisted, but in many cases they act not unlike gangsters. At any time an irrational judgment could be handed down that would land you in prison. Nonetheless, there are many things that need to be fought for regardless of the consequences.

During the Cultural Revolution someone like me might have been just up and shot. Why don't the officials dare to do that now, then? Never think that the values of the people in power have changed, nor that they have made much progress in their thinking. All the change has come from concessions they were forced to make due to the citizenry's noble efforts, sometimes won by the people even at the cost of their own freedom. As to the suppression of Falun Gong, if all citizens turn a blind eye to it, for how many years will we bear the burden of having silently consented to such an injustice? If all lawyers remain silent on it, how will their actions be viewed in the future?

So long as I have freedom, I will continue to fight for Huang Wei.

A Loner's Solitude

January 8, 2005, Beijing

I couldn't help but weep upon reading the essay, "The Lonely Solitude of Attorney Gao Zhisheng" which was written by Mr. Yuan Hongbing[9] and given to me by a friend. Mr. Yuan makes a profound and impassioned comment on the state of China's legal profession. Chinese lawyers have become numb to their social responsibilities, and their ethics are all but gone. This does need to be condemned. However, it would be unusual for a person or group to seek to bring shame to itself. I in no way disagree with Mr. Yuan or his depiction of Chinese lawyers: "China's lawyers are just like dogs, wagging their tails and begging for food from the corrupt judicial authorities."

Fellow Lawyers: Distinguish Noble From Ignoble

His essay is indeed pertinent, and I sincerely hope that my colleagues will read it. I am not too hopeful, however, of a single essay's ability to effect major change.

It addresses a topic distressing to both Mr. Yuan and me. In 2001 I handled a case that national and foreign media alike described as "the lawyers' absurd dispute." In it a renowned lawyer from northeastern China, Wang Yuqi, and I were defending Yao Zhiping, Chairman of the Yao Group. He had been falsely accused of kidnapping one of CCTV's "Focus Interview" reporters.

Mr. Wang and I met with Mr. Yao when he was in custody. He said, "I'm so grateful to you, Mr. Gao, for rushing to the Northeast all the way from Xinjiang to defend me without being offered a cent of remu-

9 A former Peking University law professor and well-known Chinese dissident now exiled in Australia.

neration. If the unjust charges against me are lifted, I'll be sure to pay both of you well to thank you. I'll pay each of you thirteen thousand dollars gratuity." I responded, "Please have confidence in and respect us as lawyers. I regard a litigant's offer to pay gratuity as a sign that he doesn't have faith in me." Tears then fell from Mr. Yao's eyes.

But Mr. Yao hadn't anticipated that Mr. Wang would necessarily recall this after the case was closed and hold him to his promise. After the case was closed, however, through various means and schemes Wang compelled Yao to give him the thirteen thousand dollars gratuity in cash, to the point where he had collected over twelve thousand nine hundred dollars from various members of the Yao family. Only sixty-five dollars had not been paid. Wang promptly sued Yao for the remaining sixty-five.

The Yao Group was framed by the CCTV "Focus Interview" reporter and others who falsified evidence. With the support of political "consultants" Mu Suixin and Ma Xiangdong, twenty administrative personnel from the Yao Group were taken into custody, ten of whom were imprisoned for approximately six months. In the course of only a few months, the up-and-coming enterprise found itself in a deathtrap. Such scheming surpasses even organized crime organizations in terms of efficiency, thoroughness, cruelty, and lethality.

Wang's demanding the rest of the gratuity via legal action was so very low and immoral. Even more distressing is the fact that five of Wang's lawyer friends testified in favor of his demand for the gratuity. Not one of them thought that Wang's demands were unjust, and all of them thought that Yao's not paying the additional sixty-five dollars was wrong!

After the hearing was over, members of the media asked me on several occasions to offer my comments on the case for the benefit of lawyers throughout China. I told my fellow lawyers that if they can draw a line between noble and ignoble acts, that will mean there is hope for the future of the legal profession. The painful reality is, though, that we are still waiting for this sign of hope!

No other profession in the world is as intimately involved in the legal system, nor takes fighting for justice as a professional duty, in the same way as lawyers. Yet in China these values are all but absent. In all fairness, though, it was not that China's lawyers as a group actively sought to bring about this state of affairs; rather, it has resulted from personal indulgence on the part of the profession as a whole. That is to say, a dog of course naturally acts like a dog, but a member of a group won't act like a dog of his own initiative. It is the group of lawyers, then, that has become this way. The problem lies in the fact that China's judicial system serves only those who go about things as dogs. This is the disturbing state of affairs that we now face.

Fighting Apathy, Loneliness Sets In

The day before I read Mr. Yuan's essay, every domestic phone call I received was from someone telling me the same thing: that I should not have written the "Open Letter to the National People's Congress." They all thought it was an extremely dangerous thing to do. I received four calls that day from family members, including one from my mother, who was in the final stages of her life. Each called to express concern over my well-being and my actions. My mother said, "Everyone knows about that injustice, as it plays out everywhere in our society. It's public knowledge. Every top official is well aware of it, but none of them dare to speak about it publicly. Why do you, an ordinary citizen, have to speak about it so publicly?" If I were to say that these reactions didn't make me feel alone, no one would believe me.

I truly appreciate Mr. Yuan's understanding. Acting independently is, in a sense, a form of solitude. But as Mr. Yuan pointed out in his essay, my lonely solitude stems from the fact that I choose to follow my own principles and go my own way. This does at times make for a painful existence, or even hopelessness. It goes far beyond loneliness.

When I have talked with friends sometimes about this pain, they've told me to rise above it all. Some have said that, with Chinese society as it is now, becoming apathetic is one way to rise above it. If you don't become apathetic, they said, then you will simply stew in your loneliness. And, more to the point, apathy can ensure one's safety somewhat. It seems that becoming apathetic to the point of heartlessness enables one to continuously benefit from the corrupt system. My lonely solitude, then, comes about because I can't help but think about the things happening in the world.

Not long ago I went to Kashgar in Xinjiang to provide legal aid to a disabled child. Two things happened there that have stuck with me. One of them occurred in the middle of the city in broad daylight: The son of an official from the Nationalities Affairs Commission savagely beat an innocent citizen. There being no outward signs of the abusive man's influential position, the police immediately went to the scene to stop him. As they attempted to carry out their duties, the hoodlum screamed, "I'm the son of ××! I dare you, you pack of dogs, to touch me! Tell whoever your supervisor is to come and see me within ten minutes. Otherwise I'll have him dismissed!"

The group of police, who had just been called dogs, then backed down in fear, and their supervisor—the local secretary of the political-legal committee—arrived immediately. The madman then began shouting in the secretary's face and went on to give the victim, who had fallen to the ground, another round of beating. So, in the end, the "People's police" were aggressively sworn at, the hoodlum son was well comforted, and the victim was taken to the hospital and monitored by the police, for fear that he might attempt to file a report upon recovery.

The other incident occurred in a meeting: A friend of mine working in the local taxation department told me that the director of the local branch of the Administration of Taxation Cai Jun, in Makit county (near Kashgar), a married man, had an affair openly with the wife of a public security policeman. After being discovered and accused by the woman's husband, Cai abused his power and made all sorts of trouble for the husband. Many of the locals are indignant about Mr. Cai's terrible conduct, but dare not speak out about it. One night, Cai Jun went to the woman's place very drunk. The doorman there was an older man, and was slow in getting the door, so when he opened it Cai beat the man to death. Cai is close friends with the head of the city's Public Security Bureau,[10] and Cai's younger brother has an important position in the police department, so he got off scot-free. He is still a government officer in that area and continues in his wicked ways.

Coincidently, after returning to Beijing I received an anonymous letter of complaint from Kashgar, and the accused was none other than Cai Jun. His behavior is itself horrible, but more horrible is how the state apparatus aids such a tyrant. It's saddening to me how quickly and routinely people forget such matters. While I have no way of changing the situation, I cannot forget it. It has all the makings of a long tragedy.

Contemplating these things inevitably leads to distress and loneliness. Many people cheer when they see the long lines outside of the studio of CCTV's "Focus Interview" program, as they think that these people finally have an outlet to share their sad stories. I don't share in their joy. Some people are delighted by the "Focus Interview" phenom-

10 The Public Security system consists of numerous bureaus, offices, and branch stations. It handles tasks such as policing and intelligence, and is often implicated in various state-run campaigns of suppression.

enon and say that is a sign of hope for China, but I see it as the complete opposite. I once wrote an article arguing that the "Focus Interview" program shows the sorry state of Chinese society—its existence indicates that the various state institutions which should handle matters for citizens are completely dysfunctional, or at least that citizens have thoroughly lost faith in them. This explains why people dismiss the entities in charge of justice in this country, but line up outside television studio doors in hopes that a show that has no obligation or ability to protect citizens' rights will solve their problems.

Having this perspective on the world is indeed painful.

The Government's Negative Influence on the Media

The media's irresponsibility and unscrupulousness is a frequent source of heartache for me.

Several years ago the Railway Ministry held a public hearing to receive comments on its proposal to raise ticket prices, and media throughout the country showed a ridiculous level of positive excitement at the proposal. It is of course perfectly lawful and justifiable for a government agency to administer such things, but the media in our country completely overemphasized the value of the move to society. In this instance the media made the officials from the Railway Ministry into national celebrities. In China, government agencies and their staff are often made into "heroes."

This phenomenon is distressing in itself, but even more distressing was the media's response to my analysis of it—they considered what I had to say dissenting opinion and refused to publish it.

In 2001, several Ph.D.'s took advantage of Hubei province's odd employment policy for talented people and thereby each accepted thirteen thousand dollars' worth of illegitimate bonuses. The government and media went wild criticizing the highly educated individuals for being dishonest and immoral. It was another display of the media's tremendous effort and craftiness in putting the government in a positive light, something beyond the imagination of media outside China.

The media invariably praised the government, excessively, for bringing in highly educated, talented people, and at the same time, rebuked the highly educated personnel for their dishonest behavior. While the criticism of their behavior was basically right, all of the media, experts, and scholars who commented on the matter named those people's poor character as the only contributing factor to the theft of taxpayers' money.

Right away I wrote an editorial to point out the following. A situation wherein individuals are able to take a large amount of government money through only slightly clever means tells us that the dishonesty lies with the government and its absolute control over taxpayers' money; our government's use of taxpayers' money is in no way transparent and constitutes absolute authority. The government seems never to have considered the risk of dishonesty in handling the money, nor taken measures to prevent it. How could they just depend on people's ethics to ensure that it would be handled properly? Many newspapers rejected the editorial, saying that it didn't represent popular opinion.

With media like this, and a society that is controlled by the media, where is there any forum to discuss real issues of honesty or ethics?

The year before last, the People's Bank of China put a new regulation in place to guard against money laundering. Within a few days, to my surprise, five experts and scholars praised the policy publicly. Truth be told, there are several flaws in the legislation, ranging from the plan for the legislation's enforcement to the technical language used.

After careful consideration and thorough research, I wrote an article about it. Yet no domestic media was willing to publish it. Surprisingly, it received high praise overseas. The Chinese media instinctively and unhesitatingly reject any voices of dissent (even ones that point out merely technical flaws) out of fear of upsetting the authorities or damaging the authorities' carefully cultivated images.

Who Will Care for Our Fellow Citizens in Need?

Not long ago, the international community generously provided aid relief to the victims of the tsunami in Southeast Asia. China's government and people weren't slack in this regard, either. I applaud the Chinese government and citizens for aiding the disaster victims.

China's celebrities were all mobilized, and the media almost blotted out the sky with its coverage of the tremendous value of such "love" and "compassion" extended by the government. My feeling about the matter was a bit different from that of the celebrities and media, however.

The disaster was something unavoidable. And yes, it's necessary to offer humanitarian aid following such a disaster, and it's natural for others to help. Aid following a disaster is something that should certainly be given; however, whether it is given should not vary based on who is on the receiving end.

China's media and celebrities are in China. The Chinese government has forcibly demolished many old homes, relocated their inhabitants against their will, and violently abused citizens' civil rights. As a result, the former inhabitants travel to Beijing to petition the central government regarding the local government's decisions. Often they are without a home and without an income in Beijing, which is a severely cold, crowded city. Their circumstances and living conditions may be far worse than that of those living in the tsunami disaster area. The tsunami and its aftermath must have been an unforgettable and traumatic experience for the victims, but for those in our society who have been forced into grave circumstances as a result of a disaster forced upon them, homelessness and lack of adequate clothing and food is something they may have to endure for the rest of their lives, or at a minimum no end to it is in sight. The greatest danger they face is not the harsh weather in wintertime, but rather the threat of being seized—and sent back home—by a cruel government official from their native city as retaliation for attempting to raise the issue with the central government in Beijing. Ironically, these same officials from their native city are also likely the ones who compelled the citizens to petition the government for help in the first place by forcing them into such bleak circumstances.

Whenever I see the media saying that "the whole nation is in high spirits" during the annual joint meeting of the National People's Congress and Chinese People's Political Consultative Congress or during the main national holidays, I can't help but think of those destitute people. Each day "the whole nation is in high spirits" is a most difficult day for them.

People such as the Falun Gong and the family members of the Tiananmen Massacre victims are monitored at those times. It has become routine for the Falun Gong believers in particular, who have been petitioning for years, to be taken into police custody on the days that "the whole nation is in high spirits." Here are a few examples: Recently, the family members of thirty-four-year-old post-doctorate Lin Yanqing from Quanzhou city in Fujian, forty-eight-year-old Wang Jinzhong from Shenyang who died tragically while in police custody, and thirty-seven-year-old Ni Guobin from Wuhan city in Hubei all wrote about this in letters they sent me. When the late Wang Jinzhong was still alive, he was taken into custody every time such a day came.

These people certainly also need the attention of the media, the compassion of celebrities, and humanitarian care and aid. However, the media and celebrities have not the slightest empathy for their own fellow citizens who are living in harsh circumstances right outside their doors. In light of this, how can one not be suspicious of the motives behind that international aid?

As I write I remember how a TV network in Germany reported on the deplorable demolition of housing near Guangzhou University not long ago. Hundreds of peasants were made homeless. Those who lost their homes built simple tents to stay in, their only shelter amidst violent storms.

The unfortunate reality is that the Chinese media and celebrities made a display of their compassion for the tsunami victims to boost their image, but couldn't care less for fellow citizens around them who are in need.

The Powerlessness of an Honest Lawyer

Professor Yuan's essay triggered a number of thoughts in me. The day before yesterday my wife asked me why no reputable company has asked me to be its lawyer despite my national reputation. As a sincere gesture in response, I gave her Professor Yuan's essay. The essay answered her very sensible question. In a society where all values are inverted, people can identify only with the inverted values, so if you are an honest lawyer they won't have faith in you. They will look merely at your "qualifications," that is, whether you have underhanded connections with the public security system, the procuratorates, and the courts. This is how lawyers in our society get ahead, so you can imagine how hard it must be for a lawyer who is committed to never using such connections… even my colleagues always sigh at me for resisting this. I'm ashamed to say it, but to this day I still can't manage to rent a presentable office, let alone purchase one, even though owning a suitable office space has always been a dream of mine.

I can't help but feel flustered at all the things I have seen. It is a known fact that some former personnel with the public security system, the procuratorates, and the court system purchase office buildings valued around 1.3 million dollars within a year after their leaving official post, yet they have never earned a law degree or passed the lawyers' exam. I happen to know a lawyer whose father was in charge of a People's High Court at the provincial level. Although his father doesn't need to appear in court even once a year, his annual income is about 1 million dollars. The lawyer told me that his father's weekly routine involves playing golf, getting facials, working out, and attending social gatherings such as dinner parties. Almost every lawyer handling a major case at his court goes to "build a relationship" with him. I know one lawyer who gave him thirteen thousand dollars at a meeting as a "consulting fee." Although I'm very aware of and familiar with the current way of doing things, every time I see what is happening I feel unsettled and as though my spirit were being destroyed! Someone like me feels meager and powerless when up against such a lawyer.

In China it is so very hard to be a lawyer who never resorts to using connections to win a case. The challenge is something most people couldn't imagine. Some local judges are blatantly hostile toward lawyers of my kind; defending low-income people in court is particularly tough. Once, after losing a lawsuit that we shouldn't have lost, the judge said openly to my client, "Simply by choosing a lawyer like him, you were condemned to lose."

I don't know who could relate to how I felt after hearing that. That sort of thing took place at all three levels of courts in Liaoning province. Many judges who have never even met me, and with whom I have no negative history, are hostile toward me simply because of my reputation for being honest.

"Building a Harmonious Society"

I was moved for some time after reading professor Yuan's essay, and my feelings led me to write this. I can say, though, having been a lawyer for seven years, that even writing a million characters could not capture even a fraction of the sorry state of our judicial system and its cruelty toward the citizens and toward civility itself.

China's leadership is making a fuss over the idea of "building a harmonious society." Usually whatever the authorities shout about the most is the thing that is in the most deplorable condition. While discovering deficiencies is not a bad thing, given the values of our current leadership, the thought of them building a harmonious society is like a foolish dream.

Ours is a society without justice; a society with no ability to address injustice; a society that has systematically brought about a huge gap between rich and poor, and between social strata; a society in which crooks control the corporate sector and knowingly exploit consumers while being protected by the system; a society without checks and balances (other than by the people's pens); a society in which individual citizens' needs do not receive the attention and respect they deserve; a society where the judicial system is unequivocally controlled by the Communist Party and the administrative authorities; a society where the power of the government is under the control of special-interest groups (and individuals), treated as a commodity, and wielded on personal whims; a society that has a constitution but continuously shuns any notion of a constitutional government; and a society in which the whole nation looks at the government's handling of the Tiananmen Massacre and the Falun Gong emotionally instead of rationally. Given all of this, isn't it beyond the capacity of any human being to build a harmonious society?

Gao and Zou Weiyi, who lost his hearing due to medical error

三

Advocating for Rights

Disabled Children

The most interesting cases I have handled, or ones warranting media attention, have been the pro bono ones involving disadvantaged groups or children who have been victimized. Everything else I've done has been business-related.

On July 15, 1998, the newspaper, *Chinese Lawyers* ran an article with the headline "Seeking Justice for a Child," which told the story of a boy named Zou Weiyi. In 1993, three-month-old Weiyi was put on an intravenous drip at the Shenyang Railway Bureau Hospital in Liaoning province. But the hospital gave him an overdose of penicillin and, as a result, he became deaf in both ears. For six years, he and his grandmother petitioned the hospital and health authorities for compensation but the hospital refused to pay even a cent. In desperation, the grandmother eventually took the child all the way to Beijing to the offices of *Chinese Lawyers* and told them their plight, which prompted the paper to publish the story I was reading. The last sentence in the article asked for help, saying: "Any lawyer in China who has a sense of conscience and would like to offer legal aid to this child, please contact *Chinese Lawyers* immediately."

As I read the article, I wept. Right afterward, I picked up the phone and called the newspaper's office in Beijing, volunteering to provide legal aid to the child. I was rather disappointed by their reply, however. They refused my offer to help, explaining that if they allowed a lawyer in Xinjiang to take the case, it would embarrass the more than 100,000 lawyers in the inland provinces.

In the end, they nonetheless chose me to represent the child. This was because each of the thirteen law firms from around the country that had offered to help insisted that the victim's family bear some of the cost; at least the travel expenses. There was only one lawyer who said that he would not take a cent from the victim, and that lawyer was me.

When the newspaper informed the grandmother about my representing the child, she refused the offer on the spot. Later, she told me that there had been two reasons for that. First, she thought that Xinjiang was too far away and she worried that she wouldn't be able to repay such a large favor. Second, because the region is underdeveloped she thought that the quality of the lawyers wouldn't be very good.

After the newspaper told me she had refused the offer, I phoned her and said, "Ma'am, this is attorney Gao Zhisheng in Xinjiang. I have a child the same age as Weiyi, and I can fully understand how you feel about the suffering the child has experienced. I would like to represent the child in this lawsuit. You'll know when you see me that I am not just trying to be nice—I can offer some substantial assistance to the child." She began to sob on the other end of the phone and said, "Mr. Gao, for so many years, nobody has called me 'ma'am' with a tone of respect, and nobody thinks that people like us have any dignity. I'll put this case in your hands."

It turned out to be a very tough case. For one thing, it meant a significant financial cost for my family. We were living in Xinjiang and the victim was in Liaoning, which was almost two thousand miles away. The plane tickets for my assistant and me would alone cost six hundred and fifty dollars one way. We didn't have much money ourselves at that time, but my wife was very generous. She said to me, "We're from poor families ourselves. It doesn't matter if this makes life a bit hard. I support you."

It was July 1998 when I took the case. Through investigations and inquiries over the phone, my assistant and I gradually obtained thirteen pieces of evidence. In early November, we decided to visit our client and file the complaint. On November 3, my assistant and I arrived in Liaoning province. We then traveled by train overnight to Dandong, the town where the boy and his grandmother lived. In order to save time, we took a specially scheduled cargo train used by small retailers. It was a bit of a mess, but very cheap.

As soon as we got off the train at Dandong, we saw an older woman holding a sign that said "Welcome, Lawyer Gao Zhisheng from Xinjiang." I was very touched. I hadn't told her exactly when I would arrive, since I didn't want to bother their family. I never expected that she would come to the station every day starting November 1 to wait for me.

I was so overcome with emotion that at the time I didn't notice the older woman's disappointment upon seeing us. Later she described to us her feelings: "I felt a natural distance from people like you who were wearing suits and leather shoes. I thought, 'Can people like this help poor people like us?'"

In Dandong, we stayed in a cheap motel that cost only two dollars per night. Mice ran back and forth along the corridor during the day. My rather frightened assistant went to the lobby and asked the receptionist, "How are we supposed to stay here with so many mice running around?" The receptionist replied with humor, saying, "Don't worry about it, Miss. There's a high school kitchen downstairs. The mice only come here during the day to find food. They couldn't be bothered to live here at night because the living conditions are too poor for them."

On November 5 we started to work intensely on the case. Before I became involved, the child's family had asked a well-known local lawyer nicknamed "Iron-Mouth Zhou" for help. He had charged them one hundred thirty dollars and filed a complaint requesting that the hospital pay one thousand dollars in damages. But after filing the case, Zhou disappeared and never followed it up, leaving the complaint unattended for years at Zhenxing District Court. Meanwhile, the hospital apparently spent twenty-one thousand dollars to hire two of the top lawyers in the Northeast to defend the case and said that they would rather spend well over a hundred thousand dollars on lawyers than pay the child one cent. After undertaking an investigation and gathering evidence, I calculated that the damages the boy deserved should be much greater than a thousand dollars. I advised the grandmother to adjust the sum sought to ninety thousand dollars (including forty thousand for pain and suffering) and filed the lawsuit with the intermediate court in Dandong.

Before the hearing, the judge said to me, "This court has never awarded more than sixty-five dollars in damages for pain and suffering. It's too risky for you to ask for forty thousand dollars. If you lose the case, covering the court filing fees and your personal expenses will be simply too much." I said to the judge, "Your advice is kind in terms of common sense, but it flies in the face of what is available by law. How do you know they shouldn't pay forty thousand dollars when you haven't heard the case?"

My assistant and I worked day and night from November 5 until the early morning of November 9 to finish preparing all the documents for the hearing. On the morning of November 9, I washed my face and went to the court.

When I arrived in court, I went to shake hands with a representative of the defendant. He was the head of Shenyang Railway Bureau's health department. I said to him, "Word has it you're able to pay well over a thousand dollars for lawyers. I'm very pleased to hear that. Too bad the days when you could behave arrogantly are over. I hope you hold on to your thousand dollars, because you'll need it when this case ends."

The hearing that day went very well. It soon became evident that we had an overwhelmingly stronger argument and that the defendant's side was feeling rather awkward. The defendant's lawyers had not prepared their case properly because they were counting on their wealth and social status to hold sway. Another factor in our favor was that three of the four judges were women. When it was my turn to speak, I described the miserable ordeals that the boy, his mother, and his grandmother had been through—running around between the State Council Petitions Office, the National People's Congress Petitions Office, the Supreme Court Petitions Office, the Railway Ministry Petitions Office, the Ministry of Health Petitions Office, and so on. As I relayed the events, sounds of sobbing could be heard throughout the courtroom.

The hearing lasted seven hours. When the boy's grandmother and I walked past a noodle restaurant during the lunch break, she said to me, "I'd like to treat you to lunch today. If you refuse to eat, that would be far too unreasonable."

I replied, "I would very much like you to treat me to lunch today. If you didn't invite me, that would be far too unreasonable. But I have one condition: That you only buy me a bowl of beef-flavored noodles, and it shouldn't cost over forty cents."

"Good, good, good!" she said happily.

When the two bowls of noodles were served, I discovered that she had ordered two extra dishes, each costing sixty-five cents. This made me uncomfortable and so I walked out. But then I worried that this would hurt her feelings, so I went back into the restaurant, got the bowl of noodles and ate it outside by the entrance.

I wasn't being overly dramatic. I did that because I knew what a dollar thirty meant to that family. For the past four or five years, they had not bought any vegetables, not even once. The local vendors all knew the family because they would go around picking up thrown-away pieces of vegetables to eat. One of the peddlers was very kind and every time he saw them, he would give them a cabbage. Later, I paid a special visit to this kind-hearted person. I told him, "You have provided some truly substantial help to that little boy. You've done something our country and government have failed to."

After the hearing was over, the boy's grandmother kindly offered to buy our train tickets to the airport, but I refused it and left twenty-five dollars for the child before we left Dandong. On the train, I received a phone call from the boy's grandmother. She was crying. It turned out that because she had insisted on taking the case to court, her daughter had left her, saying, "You won't win the case, even if you sue until you grow old and the boy grows old!" But later, when her daughter read a newspaper article about the case, she came home, knelt down in front of her mother and said, "Even Mr. Gao, who is neither friend nor family, came to support you from Xinjiang, but I didn't; I feel really unworthy of being your daughter."

The grandmother said to me over the phone, "Mr. Gao, you are really magic! You have not only helped my grandson, but also brought my daughter back to me."

Because of the defendant's powerful influence and government ties, the case took a long time for the judges to decide. Before the Spring Festival, I sent the court two faxes with some bitter remarks, complaining about the unwarranted delay. I also sent the child another twenty-five dollars, with a message that said, "'Uncle Gao' in Xinjiang is very busy, but he always remembers you in his heart."

On the eve of the Spring Festival, the boy's whole family called to tell me that a judgment had been issued and the child had been awarded fifty-three thousand five hundred dollars in damages, including twenty-six thousand for pain and suffering.

The boy's family was delighted but I was not. That's because, by law, even twice that amount of money would not adequately compensate for the suffering the boy and his family had endured. I couldn't relax and enjoy that year's Spring Festival because the case was on my mind the whole time: "If I appeal, what if the twenty-six thousand dollars for pain and suffering is overturned? But if I don't appeal, Weiyi won't get the full benefits to which he is legally entitled." At that point in time, there had actually been only four cases in China that had awarded as much as twenty-six thousand dollars for pain and suffering, and three of those were cases I had handled. Of course, there was another issue as well, which was that if I appealed, I would have to travel Xinjiang and the Northeast a few more times.

I decided to appeal. The court hearing was held on April 19, 1999, and I arrived in Shenyang on April 6. On appeal, there was a new addition to the defense team—the boy's former lawyer, "Iron-Mouth Zhou." Because the defendant offered him more money, Zhou decided to change sides and argue against his former client. I felt deep regret to see that there are such unprincipled people among lawyers.

In the end, we won the case with full success for Weiyi. The court decided to grant him one hundred and eight thousand dollars in damages, which was the highest sum ever awarded in a medical malpractice suit in China.

But the award came after over six years of appealing in court, which took a serious toll on the family's health. During those years, they had slept at stations, docks, and by the side of the road. And they had begged for food. Little Weiyi used to show me his photo collection. The photos had all been taken in front of petitions offices—that of the State Council, the Supreme Court... On one occasion, Weiyi had run a high fever, so his grandmother took him to the defendant's hospital to ask for some money for treatment. Instead of helping her, four of the hospital's security guards kicked her and the child out. What a process a victim has to go through to assert his or her rights.

When I bid farewell to the family after the case was over, something amusing happened. Weiyi's grandmother said to me, "Now the lawsuit has ended. Listen, I bought a small box of seafood for your dear wife and daughter. You must take this to them." "No problem," I said, "I'll take it to them." But before taking it with me, I insisted on opening the box even though they tried to stop me. As I had expected, there was a plastic bag in the box containing twenty-six hundred dollars. I took the money out and gave it back. Tears ran down the grandmother's face. She said, "Mr. Gao, we can never outwit you."

Justice Came to Their Aid

Zou Weiyi's case was one of the most memorable of my career. At the time, I was deeply involved in it emotionally. And even today, I'm moved when I think of everything we went through during the proceedings. Though I may have sacrificed a lot for the little boy, I gained much more in return.

The case went on for several years, so Weiyi's family and I became quite close. Even once the case was over, we stayed in touch and would telephone each other at New Year's and on other holidays. When I went to visit Weiyi and his grandmother in 2002, they showed me something that moved me to tears—they had photocopied the four money orders

I had sent for Weiyi's birthdays and had mounted them into an album to remember the help I had given them.

When I took Weiyi for an outing in Dandong, I was touched by the kindness of strangers. Since the local media had reported widely on the progress of the lawsuit, many local residents recognized us and offered assistance in their own way. The taxi driver refused to charge us for the ride. The park offered us free admission. The street vendors refused to accept money when I bought Weiyi something from their stalls. I joked with them that I should consider moving to Dandong because I would have no worries for the rest of my life.

Despite victories like the one in Weiyi's case, during the first six years of my professional career, I felt great pain because I saw no improvement in China's judicial system. When the media interviewed me after the completion of Weiyi's case, they said I should be pleased because it was the largest amount of damages awarded yet for medical malpractice in China. I told them that as far as the specific interests of the child were concerned, I was quite happy that he had been compensated. But I also said that there were other questions that needed to be asked, such as, "Why was it that before I became involved in the case, not a single department cared enough to solve the problem for the grandmother and her grandson? Why had it taken as long as six years for the judiciary to make a fair ruling in the child's favor? Why was it that when the child needed help very few lawyers came to his aid, whereas when a powerful defendant needed legal assistance, top lawyers hurried to join the fight against a disabled child?"

Zhou Chenghan Wears a Swiss-Donated Hearing Aid

The medical and health sector is rife with examples of atrocious and inhumane conduct. The main factors that give rise to such cases are the technical and financial power of the hospitals, as well as their political influence as state organs. The lack of morals or basic respect for the law in the court system further renders the handling of such cases extremely unfair. I have done my utmost over the past few years to change this situation. Because almost every case I handled was reported across the country, it has indeed helped change some people's notions of justice.

Zhou Chenghan and Zou Weiyi suffered similar misfortunes, since both their cases involved medical overdose accidents, which caused them to lose hearing in both ears. I was the attorney in both cases, but Zhou Chenghan did not make out quite as well as little Weiyi.

As with Weiyi's case, medical malpractice was to blame for Zhou Chenghan's disability. In Zhou Chenghan's case, the head of the Health Bureau personally defended the hospital in court. He stated openly in court, "We're not going to let you win. If by any chance you should win, as long as I am in charge of the health bureau, don't even think about getting a cent from us!"

Zhou Chenghan's grandmother was so disturbed by what the man said that she fainted on the spot and died a few hours later.

The lawsuit went on for about four years and was extremely difficult. When I spoke before the Supreme Court of Jilin Province, I had trouble holding back tears. I said to the judge, "Your honor, when ethics and justice become powerless in a society, when truth and conscience become powerless, then such a society has become a powerless society. Today, as we stand here under the national emblem, what is it that is truly being conveyed by this court? It is that ethics, conscience, justice, humanity, and truth have all become powerless in your hands. And instead, the Public Security Bureau, the procuratorate, the court, the hospital, the Health Bureau, the Party Committee, and the government have joined forces to fight against a defenseless, disabled child."

This was not rhetoric, but genuine sorrow.

We eventually won. It was a moving and tearful moment when the boy was awarded damages of over sixty-three thousand dollars. But, to date, although we have exhausted every avenue and all our energy, he still has not received one cent of it. This is a gross insult to those who established our laws, and to those who enforce them. The boy is now wearing a hearing aid, but it is not thanks to his mother country. Instead, it was a gift from the Swiss Ambassador in Beijing, who had read accounts of the boy's plight.

Banner Hung on a Pedestrian Overpass

One day in 1999, a friend called me and said, "There's an unusual sight on an overpass. You have to go take a look." When I got there I saw a banner hung across a busy pedestrian overpass that said "Looking for Lawyer Gao Zhisheng." Below the banner stood a couple and three children, one of them a nine-year-old boy with brain damage.

I escorted them back to my office. Their name was Wang and they were from the Altay region in northern Xinjiang. When the boy was three years old, he had developed a disease that was common among those working and living on pastures. He underwent what was supposed to be a simple operation at an army hospital, but ended up suffering severe brain damage. Afterwards the family tried many times to talk to the hospital officials and other relevant departments about the incident, but they were rejected each time. So the whole family traveled eight hundred and seventy miles to Urumqi to look for me.

I was in tears as I looked at the child and listened to their story. He was a nice-looking little boy, but because his neck had been injured, he couldn't hold up his head. His head hung over helplessly. I thought that if that had happened to my child, I wouldn't have been able to bear it.

So I put twenty-five dollars in the boy's hand and decided to take the case to court on their behalf.

Xinjiang is impoverished and underdeveloped. The judges there are known throughout China for being conservative. Still, after traveling back and forth four times between Altay and Urumqi, in the end, I managed to get twenty-one thousand dollars in compensation for the little boy.

Yang Weiguo Doesn't Live Long Enough to See Victory

I handled quite a few medical lawsuits during those years. In another case, the three-year-old son of a laborer, named Yang Weiguo, had been playing in a market one day when he saw what he thought was a bottle of mineral water at a seafood stall and drank it. It turned out the liquid wasn't water but caustic soda, which the vendor used to make the seafood look fresh. The caustic soda burned the boy's esophagus and fused it shut. The hospital worked out a plan that would involve twenty-two operations, during which they would remove the entire esophagus and then gradually pull the intestines up during each of the subsequent surgeries.

Immediately following the incident, the boy's parents went to speak to the seafood vendor. The vendor agreed to give them thirteen hundred dollars, but told them they needed to fill out an IOU so as to repay him later.

After two or three of the twenty-two operations had been completed, the boy's family was reduced to poverty and financial ruin. One of the hospital's physicians suggested they go to Xinjiang to look for a lawyer called Gao Zhisheng. The family thus came to Xinjiang and found me, without a phone number or an address, but only my name.

The seafood vendor's side had a rather strong lineup in the case, with ten defendants and twelve lawyers. On our side were only myself and the boy's father. Even before the proceedings began, the defense deliberately spread the word that they had a close relationship with the local political-legal committee, the People's Congress, and the judge. They said, "Gao wants to win this case, but he'll be attempting the impossible."

I told them at the beginning of the case, "If you've got any sense, you will compensate the child now. In that case, all you'll lose is money. But if you don't have any sense and blindly believe in the power of money, then in the end you will have lost both your money and your morals."

As with the other cases, we received a lot of public attention and support. I was giving a series of lectures to the personnel of the public prosecutor's office at the time. When they learned that I was representing the child pro bono, they assigned a car for me to use. In addition, the Xinjiang TV station followed the progress of the case from the beginning. In the end, the court decided to award the child forty-two thousand dollars in damages.

But what was most unfortunate about this case was that, because of the delay in receiving treatment, Yang Weiguo died before he could witness the victory or receive his compensation.

My clients and I won the above-mentioned lawsuits, and because we won, I'm in a pretty good position to comment on them.

What did the lawsuits tell us about China today? More than anything, we saw in our fellow Chinese the capacity to offer moral support, and we saw their sense of justice and conscience. I often mention this because this is perhaps the only remaining hope for China. As for the law, it has not demonstrated the capacity to play a role on its own. The decisions in favor of these children were usually made because of public support and pressure from the media—who closely followed and reported on the proceedings—rather than out of the judges' genuine concern for the children's rights under the law. So although the law played a role during the process, it was entirely due to the involvement of these social forces that it held any sway.

If I have any feeling of satisfaction for what I've accomplished over the past few years, it is this: I have supported many children and enabled them to receive compensation for their suffering. Sure, some of my fellow lawyers whose values are the opposite of mine say I'm "engaging in lawsuits free of charge all over China with the ferocity of a mad dog." I'd like to address those remarks. My purpose as a lawyer is not to offer free legal services; rather, offering these is something I feel I have no choice but to do. When parents bring their children thousands of miles to look for you, when you learn of the pain they have suffered, what other choice do you have? Their tears become your tears. Of course, you may feel you aren't able to truly protect them, but at minimum you can help them in the process of attempting to assert their rights. That is all.

Of course, these sorts of cases have also brought me considerable stress, especially in recent years when I have been approached, from around the country, about so many of them. No matter how "mad" I may be, I can't take them all.

A Rural Road

May 18, 2005, Beijing

Gao is known not only for assisting people through legal representation, but also for rights advocacy through publicizing people's plight. This he does by writing essays and articles and submitting them to, primarily, online publications. The following is an example of one such piece.

—Ed.

Last month, I attended a forum held at the Beijing Friendship Hotel to discuss an engineering project to prevent the water level from dropping too low at the lakes in Beijing's Old Summer Palace gardens. A number of media groups organized the forum. When it was over, a reporter asked me what I wanted to say to the government right then. I replied, "The biggest favor this current government can do people is to do nothing."

The crux of the matter is the abuse of power. There is nothing unusual about the state abusing its power in our country—it's been like this ever since day one of the current regime. The miseries that Chinese people have suffered due to the abuse of state power are too numerous to record. Ever since the Party took over and Chinese people supposedly "stood up" to become "their own masters," the number of people the regime has killed far exceeds the number of Jews killed by the fascist Nazi regime in World War II.

Interestingly, the most malicious acts of power abuse did not end with the Cultural Revolution[1] in 1976. Quite the opposite—with the blessing and protection of the entire society, such abuses have become even more prevalent. Take, for example, the forum I attended. People were freely commenting about things that skirted around the question of power abuse, and both speakers and listeners were having a jolly good time. However, when I spoke and made the point that the key issue in question was the unscrupulous abuse of state power, I was politely yet firmly cut off by the highly-alert person presiding over the forum.

The handling of Lin Zhangwang and three other "illegal" occupants of cultivated land—the case I wish to discuss here—has once again shown us just how prevalent such abuses of power have become.

Yaokeng village is part of Longquan city in Zhejiang province. It is home to twenty-six households, totaling more than a hundred people.

1 Initiated by Mao Zedong as a means to reassert power within the Party, the Cultural Revolution (1966–1976) was for many Chinese one of the most traumatic eras of communist rule.

As it is remotely located in a mountainous area, and the roads leading up to it are narrow and dangerous, the villagers are practically cut off from the outside world and live in extreme poverty. But, determined to change their fortunes, the villagers made efforts to build a road. After years of unremitting effort, they managed to raise thirteen thousand dollars. Unfortunately, after digging only a hundred yards they had to give up in the middle due to insufficient funds.

After more years of effort, on January 20, 2004, about twenty representatives from Yaokeng village entered into a contract with Lin Zhangwang and three others. According to the contract, Lin and the three others would fund the construction of a tractor road from nearby Huangta village to Yaokeng. The contract made it clear that Yaokeng's representatives would be responsible for handling policy procedures concerning forestland, compensation over farmlands and graveyards, and the clearing of obstacles, as long as these were within the territory under Yaokeng's jurisdiction. After the contract was signed, Lin Zhangwang and company raised over fifty-two thousand dollars and started to make several generations' dream come true—they began to build a road.

On April 20, 2005, when the road designed to end the villagers' generations-old isolation was about to open, the "people's" government showed up. Longquan city's forestry police substation had decided to detain Lin Zhangwang and his three colleagues under the charge of "illegal use of forestland," and took them away. Then on April 30, they formally arrested Lin under the charge of "illegal use of farmland."

From the letters I received, I learned that the police substation collected three six-hundred-and-fifty-dollar bail charges from each of Lin's three colleagues and, on the same day, further extorted a total of seventy-eight hundred dollars from them.

Judging from the materials that were sent to me along with the letters, the actions the police took were completely out of line, and the heavy fines imposed on Lin and company were outright robbery. Although lawyers and a range of people have pointed out that their actions were unlawful, the police department has refused to admit any wrongdoing. Stubbornly sticking by their wrongful actions like this is utterly ludicrous. Not only should those wrongfully imprisoned and robbed fight such openly unethical behavior, but society, as well as those in the Party and government who have any decency, should also take a stand.

While it's true that the designated use of certain farmland had changed, the way the authorities handled the matter effectively amounts to objective incrimination, which has long been condemned by legal theorists.

Before it can be determined whether a land takeover is legal, two criteria must be examined. First, were the means of land annexation legal or illegal? Second, who has come to occupy the land?

There are only two scenarios for illegal occupation and use of cultivated land. One is where the act is illegal both in terms of substance and procedure. In that scenario, people who don't have legal rights to the land occupy it by illegal means. The second scenario is one wherein the occupation is illegal only in terms of procedure—people who actually have rights to the land occupy and use it without following proper procedures. Case law over the years has indicated that it is not considered a criminal act for someone who possesses legal rights to land to occupy that land without following the relevant procedures; in that situation it is merely a question of administrative regulations, not criminal law. In the case of Yaokeng, the village has the right to arrange for the use of the land under its jurisdiction. Since the only breaches were of relevant procedural regulations, Yaokeng's case has nothing to do with criminal law.

As to the question of who the people actually occupying the land are, this is in fact very simple. We need only to determine who owns the road, as the ownership of the road depends on the ownership of the land underneath. The land in this case belongs to Yaokeng village, and therefore the road, too, surely belongs to Yaokeng. Namely, Yaokeng village has occupied its own land. Therefore, even if the act of occupying and using the land should constitute a crime, the charge should be laid against the occupier of the land, which is the owner of the road, not Lin and company, who were actually charged.

It's also worth noting that it was illegal for the police department to collect bail from Lin's three colleagues while demanding twenty-six hundred dollars from each of them at the same time. The illegal nature of such conduct is not merely a matter of failing to follow proper administrative regulations, but a typical case of abuse of power. In China, any administrative fine above one hundred and thirty dollars is considered a "substantial fine," and "substantial fines" should be imposed only by following the procedures for registration, service of summons, evidence collection, notification of rights, hearings, decisions on fines, notification of decisions, etc. What the police department did is no different from what terrible gangs do. By violating the proper procedures and extorting money from citizens, the police themselves are actually committing a crime.

I would like to stress that it's not that the act of Yaokeng village collectively using its land to build a road constitutes a crime because the land is forbidden to be put to other use. Constructing a road is a reasonable way of putting the land to effective use. It would be a completely different story if the farmland were occupied and put to some other use that would be detrimental to society. But neither Article 342 of the Criminal Code nor Article 74 include any content to the effect that using land to build a road for tractors is somehow illegal. Moreover, crimes of illegal occupancy of cultivated land are crimes committed with deliberate intent, as defined in the Criminal Code. But in this case, neither Yaokeng village nor Lin and company had any intent to deliberately commit a crime.

What's truly disappointing is the following. When generations of Yaokeng villagers lived in misery and isolation due to their natural environment, they did not receive any care or help from the government for decades. When the villagers repeatedly asked the government to help them improve their living conditions, they were simply ignored. When Yaokeng's villagers eventually raised thirteen thousand dollars to build a road, yet had to stop partway after their funds ran out, government help was still nowhere in sight. During all the years when Yaokeng village was building the tractor road and during the one-year period when investors became involved in the road's construction, the government never stopped the construction nor suggested that there was anything legally problematic about the project. Just when the dream of generations of Yaokeng villagers was about to materialize, however, the government made its timely appearance. How shameful and disappointing.

People discussing this on the Internet said, "What do those neatly-dressed officials really want?" Indeed, why are they doing this?

The Oil Investors

August 8, 2005, Beijing

In this essay Gao discusses his involvement in the prominent effort of private investors in Shaanxi province's Yulin city to seek legal redress for illegal government expropriation of oil wells. He later published an investigative report on his findings.
—Ed.

On July 12, 2005, Dr. Xu Zhiyong, Dr. Teng Biao, attorney Li Heping, and I traveled to Shaanxi province with the aim of ending the illegal detention of renowned human rights attorney Zhu Jiuhu and eleven oil-well operators. After arriving in Shaanxi, the four of us went to the Jingbian County Police Department's detention center. Although we had known for a while about the ruthlessness of northern Shaanxi's government officials, what we had heard still fell quite short of what we personally experienced.

Upon arriving at the detention center, we were chased away like chickens and dogs by the People's Police and the People's Armed Police. Even after we were hundreds of yards away from the center, the armed police officers, who were in an elated mood after their fierce behavior, wouldn't stop harassing us.

Behind us we heard the loud sounds of scurrying steps and yelling. A group of armed policemen and the head of a brigade appeared, attempting to stop us and to flagrantly impose their power. A few soldiers, who were standing on raised platforms behind the center walls, felt emboldened by their leader's domineering behavior and yelled out, "Arrest them, arrest them! Don't let any of them escape. Let's take them in and deal with them here."

We were a group of learned weaklings up against beastly armed men. As the saying goes, "When an intellectual comes face-to-face with a soldier, he'll never win the argument, even if he's right." We argued and exhausted ourselves shouting anyway, but it still took us almost half an hour before we were able to get away. After we left, I told some onlookers, "If people in suits are treated this way, you can imagine what the ordinary locals, who have to deal regularly with these gentlemen in uniform, have to put up with!"

The following morning, we spoke with a Jingbian County Police deputy for nearly two hours and, after he reported to his superiors, we spent three hours speaking with the relevant leaders of the Yulin City Political-Legal Committee and the police departments at the municipal and county levels. We engaged in regular dialogue with them for the next twenty days or so. During that period, the city and county officials who were thinking rationally gradually gained the upper hand. They came to the conclusion that it was important to release attorney Zhu Jiuhu. The message they conveyed to us was that Zhu's release was a foregone conclusion, and all that remained was the question of when he would be set free.

On July 21, the main person in charge of Yulin city's police department met with me and said that Zhu was going to be released in thirteen days, and that I should return to Beijing and wait there for further notification. On July 28, the police department told me, "Come over tomorrow," and so I returned to Yulin. The thirteen days came and went, but Zhu was still not released.

In the end, it seems that the conservative, ignorant, and uncivil forces won out; their decision was to continue unlawfully detaining innocent citizens.

Over that period of interacting with various city and county-level officials, I noticed they shared the following view: It's perfectly legal to expropriate privately-operated oil wells, just as it is to arrest lawyers and civil rights workers. They made it out as though accepting this starting point was a precondition for any further dialogue with them. I told them, "Unless you believe that whatever the authorities choose to do is automatically legal, the so-called legality you describe is nothing more than an ignorant, shabby excuse."

First, it was directly by going through their legal procedures that the private investors gained the right to run the oil wells.

Second, it's not that when the government, even the central government, wants to expropriate the property of a private enterprise it can just grant itself the right to do so by formulating some documents. It's a basic principle of modern law that property ownership can be transferred only through laws or contracts. At the same time, for thousands of years our people have shared the basic belief that it is wrong to take anything from others. Therefore, what the government has been doing goes against both basic principles of modern law and what the general public deems ethical.

Third, not having gone through any basic legal procedures, the government colluded with the police force, the procuratorate's office, and the court to arbitrarily seize the product of private investment by means of violence, kidnappings, beatings, and unlawful detention. This itself is a crime against society; there is no question of its illegality.

Fourth, government officials at three different levels—provincial, county, and city—deceived the public by saying they were "reclaiming oil wells." However, in the process, they forcibly seized not only oil wells, but also other private assets worth nearly one million dollars. These assets, which included infrastructure and facilities, are the product of ten years of work put in by the private investors. Now government officials have turned these into their own property. What law has given the government this right?

Fifth, was this reclamation of private property a legal act of government or a violent act of an underworld organization? These two are fundamentally different. I must remind the government that its relationship with any administrator should be only a legal relationship, and nothing else, unless the government is willing to openly acknowledge that it is an illegal government. If acts are to be legal, then they must follow legal procedures. Any legal government should recognize this very basic principle. When it comes to the ownership of such large-scale, huge assets, how could the government ignore and treat as worthless administrative investigative procedures, delivery procedures, notification procedures, hearing procedures, compensation procedures, adjudication procedures, and litigation procedures? The claim that their own procedures are legal is beyond ridiculous.

Sixth, the government is offering only tens of millions of dollars as compensation for assets worth approximately 1.3 billion dollars. This alone makes the government's talk of legality sound absurd.

Seventh, after the government seized the end product of some ten years of investment by thousands of investors, the victims reported this to the police department, the procuratorate, and the court, but these entities all refused to accept the complaints the investors attempted to file. From there, the situation has deteriorated to the point where, now, whoever tries to file a complaint is arrested, whoever hires a lawyer is arrested, and even the lawyer who has been hired is arrested. Such odious behavior is a slap in the face of everyone in the nation who seeks rule of law, and amounts to openly undermining the central government's proposed goal of "building a harmonious society." There is nothing legal about any of this.

Eighth, they used huge amounts of money to bribe the Chinese Communist Party's Ministry of Propaganda—civilization's public enemy—to crack down on domestic media that was trying to report objectively. Three different levels of government organized a huge team that traveled to Beijing five times in order to bribe various central government departments. This clique also openly threatened Professor Guo Haiyan, who spoke out to uphold justice, and other specialists and scholars in the capital. In addition, they openly rejected lawyers' requests to meet with their detained clients. Where in modern legal history can you find any precedent for calling such reactionary, vicious acts legally legitimate?

What's interesting is that later, when we contacted these local officials, they all changed their statements about the legality of their seizing the oil wells—from at first claiming that their actions were legal to later saying they had been approved by the central government. In today's era, civilized societies use the law, not possession of political clout, as the standard for judging whether a certain action is right or wrong.

China's central government doesn't have the right to place itself above the law, even though it has been brutishly doing so all along, as everyone knows. If a civilized society's standard for judging right from wrong is indeed none other than the law, then what kind of justification is "approved by the central government"? Is something correct and legal simply because it is "approved by the central government"? I don't see how anyone could accept this idea, unless perhaps these officials' minds are still bloated with the idea that the Chinese Communist Party is forever "great, glorious and correct."

Besides, as we have seen, what is "approved by the central government" is far from being always correct. For instance, the central government approved the Great Leap Forward,[2] as well as the Anti-Rightist Campaign[3]—campaigns the likes of which had never before been seen. The central government approved the Suppression of Counterrevolutionaries Campaign,[4] and it then approved over ten brutal campaigns of struggle between different groups in the Communist Party. The Cultural Revolution was approved by the central government, as was the 1989 Tiananmen Massacre, the campaign to persecute our fellow countrymen who believe in Falun Gong, and the list goes on.

Clearly, it's not the case that if something is approved by the central government it is automatically legal and correct. Quite the opposite. Despite existing laws and regulations, the central government has used its power to approve matters that are in open violation of the constitution, law, and the principle of rule of law. It also clearly shows that the central government doesn't pay even the slightest attention to the constitution and law. This is the reality we have been facing for over half a century.

2 An economic and social plan launched by Mao Zedong in 1958 meant to rapidly develop China's economy. The plan proved disastrous, leading to famine that claimed an estimated 30 million lives.

3 A Maoist campaign enacted in the 1950s and early 1960s wherein intellectuals were criticized, terrorized, and persecuted for exercising independent thought and speech.

4 A Maoist campaign in the early 1950s targeting mostly those associated with the former Nationalist government, secret societies, and religious groups. The death toll is thought by some to be as high as 2 to 3 million.

The fact that three levels of government in Shaanxi province chose to continue detaining innocent lawyer Zhu Jiuhu and others clearly indicates that the only option in the mind of the interest group involved is to continue acting in a cruel, reactionary, and barbaric way. The long sessions of negotiations and the final result gave us once again the opportunity to see, up close, that this clique is extremely efficient and energetic when it comes to doing evil. When it comes to choosing civil, legal, and moral ways, however, it is extremely feeble.

Several of the oil investors who had protested the government's expropriation have since been indicted by the Jingbian County Procuratorate.

—Ed.

The Spiritual Group

The government's flagrant persecution of our fellow countrymen who practice Falun Gong has continued for six years since it began on July 20, 1999. As the sixth anniversary approaches, Falun Gong practitioner Hao Qiuyan from Shijiazhuang city has been unlawfully detained for over half a year now by the local government, and her husband Huang Wei, who also practices Falun Gong, is being unlawfully detained as well. This is the second time the local government has detained Huang Wei; he has suffered in detention for over five of the past six years. This is the current reality and there has yet to be any sign of change.

Both the young husband and wife have a good university education, and those who know them speak highly of the two. Ever since meeting them separately, the qualities that they both exhibited—calmness, well-cultivated character, magnanimity, and faith in living a noble life—have lingered in my memory.

When talking with them, one senses that they aren't down on society, despite having been persecuted. When speaking with Huang Wei, I was brought to tears by his deep and tender feelings for his family. He told me that whenever he heard the sound of children playing outside the high detention center walls, he would close his eyes for a long time and imagine the happy scenes of being with his wife and child. When he talked about his parents and his in-laws, I saw tears in his eyes. He told me he was pained not because he could not show filial piety toward them, but because it was his and his wife's income that had kept the entire family going. Both his and his wife's parents are elderly and in poor health. They don't have enough income even to take care of their basic needs. In addition, because of the young couple's detention, the grandparents now have to look after their young child. Huang said he would never understand how the government could benefit from detaining people like him or his wife. He told me, "Long-term detention is a huge disaster for us and for our families, and it offers no benefit to the government. Moreover, such detention violates the Chinese constitution and basic legal principles."

In today's China, as many as one hundred thousand Chinese citizens who practice Falun Gong have been held in long-term detention like Huang Wei and his wife.

In February, I carried out a fact-finding investigation into the government's persecution of the Falun Gong, which has brought harm to the people since 1999. The facts are stifling. What I found so truly horrifying was not only that such atrocities, which are offensive to God, had taken place, but that you could really feel and see that those disasters were continuing. Not long before we arrived in Yantai city, which looks rather nice on the surface, another ten innocent Falun Gong believers were arrested and sentenced. The reason for their arrest and sentencing? Someone had posted on the Internet a list of the names of the wicked perpetrators who persecute Falun Gong people. The local government became panic-stricken, as if faced with a formidable enemy. Therefore, in the name of "national security," it began carrying out large-scale arrests, and a group of Falun Gong adherents who had long been labeled as "stubbornly resistant to being 'transformed'" were once again put into prison.

For Chinese citizens, especially those who practice Falun Gong, their personal freedoms, and even their very lives, are under constant threat; as soon as the authorities feel a little "unsafe," these persons may face disaster. The history of our current regime reveals that whenever the authorities or a particular leader feels unsafe—regardless of whether this feeling has any basis in reality—the habitual reaction is to arrest a large number of people from the group being perceived as a "hostile force." This is known as "eliminating unstable elements in their embryonic stage." Whenever the authorities feel fearful or construct some kind of assumption about a particular group, they arrest people. In today's China, the days on which the authorities do not feel fearful are few and far between. Thus, very few days in a year pass without mass arrests.

What has really made people feel desperate and helpless in recent years is the way in which the authorities have been using any possible excuse to arrest Falun Gong believers. Hao Qiuyan was arrested simply for trying to obtain legal representation to deal with her husband's wrongful imprisonment; the explanation for her arrest was that she not only "refused to be transformed," but was also "very active." Hao Qiuyan is still jailed. Some Falun Gong practitioners were detained and interrogated, even beaten and tortured, simply because they had agreed to cooperate with my investigation. Several practitioners' homes were savagely ransacked just a few hours after I interviewed them. Because of all this, I was left with no choice but to end the investigation with a pained heart.

This regime's twisted undertaking of brutally suppressing people of faith is not something that started a mere six years ago. However, the cruel nationwide persecution of Falun Gong believers has seen no precedent both in terms of the number of people unlawfully detained and killed, and in terms of the degree of brutality. Six years have passed, and yet there is still no sign of even a modicum of good intent on behalf of local governments to abandon their evildoings and change for the better. The ongoing unlawful detention of Huang Wei and his wife, along with the simultaneous arrest of twelve Falun Gong practitioners from Yantai and another six from Chongqing, is the latest confirmation that local governments refuse to stop doing evil and to act humanely.

Although Falun Gong practitioners have been suffering for six years under an inhuman officialdom that refuses to stop persecuting, this period of time has seen some changes. More and more people around me, including professionals, scholars, government staff members, and ordinary Chinese citizens have begun to question the rationale behind the campaign against these believers. This has been a palpable change: People used to keep dead silent when it came to Falun Gong, but now, calling into question the government's persecution of Falun Gong practitioners has become a natural topic of conversation for more and more people. These people have come to realize how unjust, inhumane, and lawless the government's violent persecution of the Falun Gong people is. This rapid, widespread change in attitude stands in stark contrast to the government's static, outdated practices. It is really quite thought-provoking.

Well-known progressive thinker Guo Feixiong has written an article titled, "To Trample Freedom of Religion Is to Trample the Heart of Human Civilization." Over the past twenty years, the state of Chinese society, as well as Chinese people's ways of thinking and concepts, have undergone great changes and are now completely different from what they were during the Cultural Revolution. This is undeniable. The gloomy reality is that the current clique that is in power still uses the outdated means adopted during the Cultural Revolution to control our society. The whole world should recognize this.

Over the past six years, what the Chinese people have witnessed is another Cultural Revolution-style campaign—an organized, systematic and persecutory campaign. The government, through its terror organization—the 6-10 Office—persecutes tens of millions of Falun Gong practitioners with a policy of "ruining their reputation, cutting off their sources of income, and destroying them physically." They unscrupulously arrest, beat, detain, fire, and punish Falun Gong believers and try to force them to "transform." They usc thc entire state machinery to spread deceptive propaganda, imposing their misconduct upon the whole nation, creating hatred, and trying to force the Chinese people as a whole to oppose Falun Gong.

The 6-10 Office is similar to the Party's notorious "Central Cultural Revolution Group" and is a Gestapo-like organization. It possesses special powers to control and manipulate all levels of the Party and administrative departments, the courts, the labor camps,[5] the public security and national security systems, and all media in China. The 6-10 Office is the headquarters overseeing the systematic persecution of Falun Gong by means of state terrorism. It orders local police stations to brutally torture, sexually assault, and even murder Falun Gong practitioners, while it also orders political-legal committees across the country to set up brainwashing centers for the purpose of forcibly "transforming" those Falun Gong adherents who refuse to give up their spiritual practice. The effort to establish rule of law in China, a project sufficiently

5 Labor camps are used by the Party to detain and punish individuals accused of a variety of offenses, many of them petty or vaguely defined. Individuals can be sentenced without trial for up to three years of "rehabilitation" or "reeducation" there. The camps are often the sight of torture and other abuses.

botched in its own right, has now been thrown into total chaos by the establishment of the 6-10 Office.

As the persecution of Falun Gong reaches its six-year anniversary, it is necessary for us to use various means to speak up about the facts we know. The purpose of speaking up is not simply to criticize the government (not that the government does not deserve criticism). Rather, speaking the truth and facing what has taken place—or what is still taking place—is absolutely necessary if ours is to be a civilized society that resolves disputes with rationality. Our government is trying to put the idea of "building a harmonious society" into practice. But until this disastrous and shameful situation that involves tens of millions of people who practice Falun Gong comes to a complete end, that wish will remain only a dream.

To declare war against people's faith is a stupid thing to do, as this is no different from declaring war against humanity. There has never been a force in history that has successfully vanquished humanity, nor will there be one in the future. Six years ago, those who are persecuting Falun Gong stupidly decided to take evil actions to fight humanity, and yet, humanity has never been defeated by any power, no matter how mighty. Factually speaking, the persecution of Falun Gong has already failed. Rather than continuing along this failed course, it would be better for the persecutors to return to the track of humanity, face reality, and do one or two humane things instead of continuing to view humanity as an enemy.

In this campaign that began six years ago and is still being carried out by all local governments, those who have suffered persecution and mental torment are not only the tens of millions of Falun Gong believers and their families. All the people of China, and even all the people of the world, are victims. It is a type of intangible injury sustained from being on the receiving end of all the lies used to bolster the persecution. The whole truth will become known in the near future. And, in the process of learning the truth, governments and people around the world will realize how their morality, mental well-being, financial economy, and more have incurred tremendous losses.

We have a responsibility to let the world know the truth.

Forced Sterilizations

January 5, 2006, Beijing

In 2005, blind activist Chen Guangcheng attempted to sue officials in Shandong province who had carried out forced abortions and sterilization operations on thousands of women—actions that were illegal even under China's one-child policy. Local authorities retaliated. By the time Gao wrote the following piece, Chen had been under house arrest for nearly four months.

—Ed.

Shandong province is powerful, very powerful.

Shandong's power stems from its position along China's coast. From the latter half of 2005 to today, the province has been fighting a virtual war against a blind man. Through the story of this war, the coastal province's "supremacy" has shone through for all to see.

On October 4, 2005, prominent human rights activist Dr. Xu Zhiyong and attorney Li Fangping set off for Shandong hoping to offer legal assistance to Chen Guangcheng. For months Chen had endured an all-out siege led by the Communist Party Committee of Shandong. The committee's efforts to keep Chen down were not unlike the level of force used when the People's Liberation Army was battling to gain control of China! The Shandong authorities keenly recognized the significance of the activist and attorney's trip to the area and therefore made meticulous arrangements to keep them out. They organized a group of local officials and thugs to be on high alert for battle. As Xu

Zhiyong and Li Fangping were on their way to help Chen Guangcheng, the group launched a swift and sudden attack, beating the two to the ground before taking them to the local police station. The next day, police escorted them back to Beijing.

In history, wars launched by militant groups have typically been for the purpose of plundering wealth. Wars that the Chinese Communist regime wages against individuals, however, are somewhat different in that they're usually launched after the people are savagely robbed, and when the victims decide to stand up and assert their rights. The recent Taishi Village Incident and the Shanwei Massacre,[6] as with the Party's war against the blind man in Shandong, all have this in common.

The roots of the Shandong "war" lie in the Party's evil, long-term practice of relentlessly disregarding people's dignity. In 2005, the Shandong authorities carried out one of their savage campaigns of forcibly, and brutally, sterilizing women (through tubal ligation), thus once again bringing misery to people. This practice of theirs, which is an affront to heavenly principles and to people's feelings, aroused the attention of Chen Guangcheng, who was well-known locally for his human rights activism. He then conducted a fair investigation, which drove the lawless government crazy. In order to cover up the crimes they committed against the locals, the authorities responded to Chen with more oppression—they put human and financial resources, province-wide, into doing battle against this blind man.

The virtual war, whose end remains nowhere in sight, and which the whole world is watching, is giving the outside world a glimpse into the coastal province's "power."

In this war against a blind individual, the government's efficiency in putting the mechanism of the state to work, and in making swift use of

6 Both were episodes in which rights violations by Party officials led to demonstrations by local residents and bloody police crackdowns.

its tools of violence is indeed quite amazing. In order to "defeat" Chen, Shandong province has brought every one of its resources into play.

In fact, all levels of government and Party committees, as well as participating work units, have gotten involved. This has included the civil affairs departments, Public Security Bureau offices, neighborhood committees, the education sector, the communications sector, and others.

The police force and local government have been the main ones responsible for carrying out the more "technical" aspects of the war, such as by beating people, arresting people, besieging people, and threatening people. These are the autocracy's lowest-level goons, and they have no problem completing whatever dirty task their superiors assign them.

But the education sector's performance has been particularly notable. Education representatives from the government went to the primary school where Chen Guangcheng's two little nephews were studying and ordered the school to expel the two little boys because "Chen Guangcheng is a counterrevolutionary."

The provincial leadership, meanwhile, has been mainly responsible for the war's more "structural" elements, such as cutting off electricity, impounding computers, manipulating equipment to render mobile phones dysfunctional, stopping all mail correspondence to and from the "enemy," and cutting off all forms of external support; the post office has even withheld food, such as powdered milk, that people sent Chen Guangcheng.

In this war between a province and a blind man, the cooperation between government agencies has been seamless!

This is an extremely mean and dirty war, both in terms of its objectives and its tactics. Still, the powerful side in this war, a province that is an economic giant, cannot seem to win. The war has lasted over a year now, yet Shandong has been unable to claim absolute victory over my blind friend. The province's efforts alone testify to the weight that justice carries, as Chen had aimed to take those in charge of the forced sterilizations to court. What's more, this has allowed people to see more clearly the frailty and breakdown of an autocratic state apparatus that once seemed so powerful. It has demonstrated that, no matter how powerful evil may seem in this day and age, when the light of justice is shone on it, it is sure to shrivel and fall.

At this point we can't see how the war against Chen Guangcheng will end. However, the result was crystal clear from the very beginning. Shandong's Party committee and government are bound to be defeated and Chen Guangcheng is bound to win. The reason is simple—how could wickedness overcome the will of Heaven?

The Petitioners

December 29, 2005, Beijing

This essay describes the danger Chinese citizens face on attempting to petition the government over their grievances, despite the petitions system being a part of China's political and legal framework. According to a 2004 study conducted by Professor Yu Jianrong, over fifty percent of petitioners surveyed said they had been beaten by state agents in the process of petitioning.

—Ed.

The Chinese Communist Party, the self-proclaimed ruling party, is constantly on pins and needles, fearing someone will topple it. It has become so irrational that it even believes some people possess some sort of paranormal knack for sabotaging its power. It believes people with these supernatural abilities can stir up trouble at any time, even when they are asleep. Terrified, the Party thus monitors you twenty-four hours a day!

Actually, like all bloodthirsty, greedy, and brutal dictatorships, the Party doesn't need anyone to topple it. That's because in the process of operating its state machinery, the Party is rapidly producing new enemies. This seems to be an internal pattern shared by all short-lived dictatorships throughout history. The more despotic the regime, the shorter its lifespan; this is one of history's irrefutable laws. The mere fifteen-year reign of the ruthless Qin dynasty should serve as ample warning. History has proven that the only lasting system of governance is one that emerges from the will of the people, one that safeguards freedom and democracy, adheres to the rule of law, and respects human rights.

A few days ago, as some sixty Shanghai residents who had petitioned the government were leaving my office, I was so pained and couldn't help shedding tears as I watched their figures recede into the bitter cold. It took me a long time to calm down, and sad scenes kept flashing through my mind. I saw the feeling of helplessness in the eyes of Du Yangming, an older man, and in his trembling hands as he tried to button up his thick coat when leaving my office. I thought about the adverse circumstances they were facing in the severe winter and about how they might be arrested at any moment...

Of these sixty or so men and women, only three or four hadn't been subjected to illegal forced labor; the rest had all suffered this cruel form of treatment at the hands of the Shanghai "people's" government!

An official Shanghai municipality document from 2005 brags of the local government's achievements, saying it had "seriously dealt with illegal behavior during petition activities."

But here are some additional facts. Shanghai resident Gong Haomin has been petitioning for ten years without any success. Shanghai residents Zhu Donghui, Wang Qiaojuan, and Xu Zhengqing have become poverty-stricken because their homes were demolished against their will.[7] Because they went to Beijing to file a petition, they were sentenced to labor camps and are still being detained. Zhu Donghui was stripped naked, handcuffed, and hung up in the air for three days and nights until he lost consciousness. The persecutors poured cold water on him and cruelly tortured him by striking his genitals…

Zhou Ronghua is an honest and quiet citizen. One morning at 3:00 A.M., a group of laborers broke into his house to illegally demolish his house. They tied up his mother and beat him up. In protest, he poured petrol on himself to try to ward off the perpetrators and rescue his mom. But he didn't actually intend to set himself on fire. He was nonetheless sentenced to a year of forced labor for the crime of arson…

According to incomplete statistics, more than seventy people in Shanghai have been detained for petitioning against forced demolition alone. Some of these people have been detained numerous times, such as Shen Yongmei, whose house was demolished without any legal procedure and who is now homeless. Many more have been sent away, put under surveillance and house arrest, and have fallen ill due to maltreatment.

Some petitioners were even sent to mental hospitals by the government as retaliation, which is even more despicable. Instead of being "treated," they were turned into actual mental patients because of drugs and injections… Sun Dongshui, seventy-five, was admitted by force to a psychiatric center in Fengxian county as soon as he refused to accept the unlawful demolition of his house. On March 28, 2004, his family was told that his former workplace would be taking care of Sun's funeral arrangements.

---

7 In recent years many Chinese residents have faced forced eviction and the demolition of their homes, often the result of local officials having been bribed by developers. Few are given fair compensation, if any.

Today I finally have time to sit down and read their complaints, written and signed with their blood and tears. These are their words:

"I am Dong Chunhua, and am nearly seventy years old now. Because we refused to accept the authorities' unlawful act of demolishing our house, my husband Cai Xinhua, who is seventy-two, went to Beijing to file a petition. As a result, he was unlawfully detained for thirteen days before being escorted back to Shanghai. The day he returned home, however, he suddenly died from unknown causes. In July 2004, my youngest daughter, Cai Wenjun, also petitioned in Beijing and was therefore detained by officers from Shanghai's Changning Police Substation. Later, when she went to the Shanghai Petitions Office to seek administrative redress, she was sentenced to one year of forced labor under the charge of 'making trouble.' Today, she's still being detained at the Shanghai Qingpu Labor Camp."

The above is from the materials Dong Chunhua, an older woman, had put together for me, titled, "A Complaint from a Veteran Communist Party Member."

"I am Liu Hualin, and am a lecturer at the University of Shanghai for Science and Technology. On February 22, 2004, I was on my way to Beijing to file a petition, but was stopped on the platform by a colleague and officials from the Shanghai Petitions Office... I was beaten to the ground. Then, a few of them pulled me up and shoved me into a taxi. I was then locked in the university president's office for the entire night... The next day they took me to the police department. I was interrogated for fifteen to sixteen hours... Throughout the whole process they didn't present any legal documents concerning my arrest or detention. At midnight, a police officer surnamed Xie told me that they would put me into administrative detention for 'interrupting official business.'… I was sentenced to 548 days of forced labor. During my detention I was fired from my job, my house was demolished, and my personal belongings were stolen, including a piano, a computer, and all my money. During the 548 days of forced labor I was tormented by anguish, humiliation, and helplessness. I've taught countless students, but how many of them believe that their teacher is innocent and that their government is unlawfully detaining their teacher?"

Du Yangming, the older gentleman, tells his story as follows:

"In April 2003, I went to the Zhabei District Petitions Office with a referral letter, but was detained for a month on the fabricated charge of: 'Gathering people together like a mob to attack a governmental department'… I will never forget what happened in the wee hours of April 25. I was tied to a bed in the Shanghai General Prison for twenty hours and, as a result, had to relieve myself in bed and lie in my own excrement and urine. It was most humiliating and a shame to all men. The previous day, certain powerful people in the district government used administrative tactics to cite me with fabricated charges… Most unacceptable was how they forcibly placed me, an honest citizen, into prison without producing any legal document or telling me on what charges I was being imprisoned.

"…I was later sent to the Dafeng Farm where I began a year-and-a-half long humiliating life of forced labor. We were given stale vegetables to eat, and the water we drank was from a deep well with insects floating in it. We were forced to do drilling work under the scorching summer sun, or simply stand in the sun as a form of punishment. In the severe winter we were forced to sit outside, exposed to the cold. We were often beaten or shocked with electric batons for no reason.

"On the evening of November 3, 2004 I was taken to the Zhijiang Police Station… I was given only three small cups of water per day (being diabetic, I needed much more water to drink). From day three on, they started giving me only one small cup of lukewarm yellowish water, which was poured out from a special thermos. After drinking the water I began feeling strange and became anxious and irritable… One instructor yelled at me, saying my life wasn't even worth as much as that of a dog if I died."

Tian Baocheng and his wife sent me their complaint, which was dozens of pages long. It was very painful to learn of the inhumane sufferings they had experienced in recent years. Here is a little bit of what Mr. Tian had to say:

"I went to petition the government but was incriminated with fabricated evidence. In order to protest severe human rights abuses I went on a hunger strike for the next two days. On April 27, 2003, I was forcibly handcuffed and taken to the Shanghai Prison hospital…

"When my detention term concluded on December 2, 2003, a guard escorted me out to the building for forced labor. He verbally informed me, 'You have been sentenced to one year and three months of forced labor'… I asked many times for proof of my being sentenced to forced labor, but all they said was, 'The authorities told us to detain you here. We don't care about anything else.'

"Two police came to negotiate with me. They said, 'You and your wife have two options: One is that you surrender unconditionally and we'll release you. The other is that you insist on seeking justice; if you do that, you will stay in prison. It's up to you what course you follow…'

"On another occasion the head of the Zhabei Petitions Office, Ye Ming, came to the detention center and roared at us, 'Damn you! You'd better be clear that you're asking for trouble! The only way out for you is to unconditionally surrender. Otherwise, you'll be imprisoned till you die.'

"On June 22, it was very hot and stuffy, so I picked up a piece of paper and fanned myself with it. But a guard surnamed Liu accused me of refusing to obey discipline and started beating me. While hitting me, he said, 'So, you won't give in and you'll file a complaint about me, right? Go ahead! You're not the only person I've beaten. There have been many others. So what! I'll bring the detention inspector here in the afternoon. Go ahead and complain about me. Let me tell you, you'll suffer more in the future.'

"The next day I reported this to Sun Guoqing, the deputy head of the guards, and asked to see the detention center director. Sun Guoqing took me to his office. As soon as we stepped in, he started punching and kicking me before I could even say anything. While beating me, he said, 'You know what this place is! You have no right to speak here. What's wrong with beating you?' I was beaten to the ground. He stomped me with his foot. I was in such pain that I started yelling, 'The police are beating me!' Sun Guoqing ran to the bathroom next door, grabbed a toilet-cleaning scrub and thrust it into my mouth. He yelled, 'So you're shouting. Let's see you shout!' This knocked out my two front teeth… Mr. Gao, my children are these policemen's age, and yet I was beaten to the point that I was rolling on the ground like a child!"

Some may say I always disturb people's tranquil lives and always rock the boat. But these reports are soaked with the blood and tears of our fellow countrymen! The people who have long become indifferent and numb are again busying themselves with preparations for grand New Year get-togethers. My wife has reminded me that many people are at this very moment busy receiving presents and goods, and that most people are intoxicated with happiness stemming from large bonuses they received ahead of the New Year.

Mr. Du Yangming said something that really struck me. He said:

"The Chinese people were originally very reasonable. After each disaster in which our families were broken up and our loved ones killed, we wiped away the tears and bloodstains, buried the bodies, and felt sincerely grateful to the disaster makers—the Communist Party. Then we waited patiently for the ever-delayed reparations. And year after year we hoped for supernatural beings to come to our rescue, for Deng Xiaoping, Jiang Zemin, and Hu Jintao to become wise, and for kinder policies toward the waves of petitioners.

"But now I don't hope for anything. I just want human rights! This is because if I accepted any material compensation from the regime today, it could take it away tomorrow. We want a government that will never rob its people, arrest, or persecute people at the slightest provocation. The regime we have is a shit regime, and we absolutely don't want such a heartless, inhumane regime. All petitioners are now like this—what we want is not to have this or that problem resolved; what we want is a government that treats its people like human beings! I say to them, 'We're not afraid of you arresting us. You've arrested me over ten times. Have I ever shown any fear?'"

Self-appointed Communist Party, listen for a moment. Given that you already have wolfish local governments like the one in Shanghai, is it really necessary for anyone to subvert your power? Everywhere across China, terribly cruel and wicked local governments are earnestly and fanatically working overtime to topple your regime!

The Shanwei Massacre

December 14, 2005

On December 6, 2005, paramilitary police opened fire on villagers in Dongzhou village of Shanwei city (located in Guangdong province), killing dozens. The villagers were protesting the confiscation of their land, which was seized without fair compensation.

—Ed.

An Internet posting about the recent incident in which the regime gunned down innocent people in Shanwei stated the following: "This is a brutal regime that from day one has always resorted to killing people to maintain its power." Everyone on the planet knows this to be true!

However, people often explain its slaughter by saying, "The regime felt that, because it hadn't killed people for a while, the people had become more bold and defiant of its rule. So the regime felt it had to kill, and the killing is both a reflection and a resurgence of its murderous nature." People have this kind of mindset, and this prevents them from clearly seeing what's happening in China today.

There's another explanation for the recent incident. Our rulers have never stopped killing people. It's merely that over a certain period of time their killing strategies were different from those carried out in Shanwei, where they killed in broad daylight.

For fifteen days, I sealed myself off and traveled to the northeastern city of Changchun to investigate the ways in which this regime, which has never stopped killing, is now savagely persecuting Falun Gong believers. I think I know our current regime quite well, but my understanding of it is now deeper. During those fifteen days, I cut off all direct contact with the outside world, including with my family. I resumed some of these contacts on only December 12, after the open letter revealing the findings of my investigation was published. During those fifteen days, another one hundred or so fellow countrymen died in mining disasters. During those fifteen days, another one hundred or so petitioners—people who no longer have the most basic living conditions because of abuse from local officials—were arrested in Beijing alone. During those fifteen days, a cold-blooded incident took place in Guangdong province's Shanwei, in which the government murdered our defenseless countrymen.

To be honest, since in today's society we hear of killings so often, the reaction of shock and sadness that I had has long since left me. How terrible! But I do feel indignant—in this society and under such circumstances, this has become my habitual reaction.

As I said, our government has never stopped murdering people. The incident in Guangdong, where dozens of citizens who peacefully petitioned their government over compensation for land seizure were shot dead, took place in broad daylight. It therefore provoked feelings of shock and indignation in some people. This is normal. The investigation that we recently undertook, however, shows that over the past six years this regime has killed at least three thousand of our fellow countrymen in its terrible persecution of Falun Gong practitioners. Actually, most people, particularly those in intellectual circles, know very well the reality of the continuous killing; it is only that the ways they react and express themselves vary greatly.

I saw eight specific demands addressed in "An Open Letter Concerning the Bloodshed in Shanwei," which I signed. But the core principle underlying these eight demands demonstrates that those in China who still have a conscience are currently in a helpless and confused state. They are recognizing the legitimacy of a regime that has just perpetrated an act of killing, and urging that same regime to investigate and deal with the legal consequences of the killing. This is a most helpless and feeble form of outcry on the part of my fellow Chinese. Everyone must realize that having perpetrators who have just committed murder to then go and investigate and rectify the situation would be both immoral and illegal.

Some may say that in a hopeless situation this is all that can be done. But here is another of the letter's distressing underlying principles: A distinction is drawn between the conduct of those in the central government and that of the specific local government agents who actually carried out the killing. Surprisingly, the central government hasn't demonstrated its usual "clear-headedness" and taken advantage of this line of reasoning. Instead, comrade Wu Bangguo[8] immediately rushed to Guangzhou to inspect the work and, evidently, affirmed the "achievements" of the local authorities. He found a most simple way of showing the people both inside and outside China that the two ruling entities are, in fact, partners.

In fact, they have always acted together. It was natural for them to act in accord at a time when the local government had just committed a massacre and was being condemned for its brutality. So the central government wanted to make absolutely certain that its comrades, who had killed dozens of people over the two entities' common interests, would not feel isolated or be criticized. It therefore promptly dispatched the Chairman of the National People's Congress Standing Committee, Wu

8 Chairman of the National People's Congress Standing Committee since 2003.

Bangguo. This individual then chatted and joked with the local leaders, who had just returned from the scene of their crime, making them feel just as credible and worthy of respect as usual, despite their having just murdered dozens of people. The little bit of fear and anxiety they had felt earlier quickly dissipated. This reassuring visit, in fact, was the central government's most prompt and direct response to the open letter we had signed!

In my own latest letter to the central government, I expressed that the current regime has been brutal, stupid, and lawless for as long as its history. Well, the Chinese people have been helpless, naive, and confused for just as long! The current regime is not qualified—in terms of morality or justice—to deal with the killing that it had itself underhandedly directed. As soon as the local government temporarily stopped killing, the regime began, with the full backing of the state-run media, to demonize our fellow countrymen who had been robbed of their property or whose loved ones were killed. It also started carrying out large-scale arrests. This is all the regime has ever known. How could we Chinese people ever forget the horrifying terror of the aggressive and unbridled arrests of "troublemakers" that took place following the 1989 Tiananmen Massacre?

Let's each begin doing something useful in our own area—let's use every possible means to encourage people to publicly withdraw from this murderous clique, to no longer help the murderers do evil, and to no longer be used as the murderers' tools! Let us peacefully put this murderous clique to an end by severing our ties to the Chinese Communist Party! Let's completely free ourselves from this disastrous misfortune!

四

Open Letters for Justice

Open Letter to the National People's Congress

December 31, 2004

To the Standing Committee of the National People's Congress and Committee Chairman Wu Bangguo:

I am a lawyer and have recently received many requests to help Falun Gong adherents who have been sentenced to forced labor camps. On December 26, my associate and I traveled to the city of Shijiazhuang in Hebei province in order to offer legal assistance to one such person, Mr. Huang Wei. In the course of raising his case with the administrative and judicial authorities, we discovered unimaginable phenomena. As an attorney and citizen, I must say these phenomena are utterly disturbing. The first thought that came to mind after negotiating with several Shijiazhuang courts was that I must act on my concerns by writing as soon as possible to the Standing Committee of the National People's Congress ("NPC") and Chairman Wu Bangguo.

In 2003, I submitted three separate requests through registered mail to the NPC Standing Committee, but they all yielded the same outcome: no reply. After thorough consideration, I decided this time to instead write an open letter.

Huang Wei, a resident of Shijiazhuang with a college education, was sent to a forced labor camp in 1999 for three years after being charged with "using an evil cult[1] organization to undermine the implementation of the law." By the time he was released at the age of thirty-four, half his hair had turned grey. Still, with remarkable diligence and perseverance he opened a small business that was off to a promising start. Though poor, his family was determined to forget the bitter past and be optimistic about the future.

At 7:30 A.M. on April 13, 2004, Huang took his child to kindergarten as usual. Once he left the kindergarten to go to work, four unidentified people abducted him. Without producing any documents, his captors sent him to the local National Security Bureau office and from there to a detention center.

Another thirty-eight days went by and he was still given no explanation for the detention. When he asked his captors which government department they belonged to, the reply they gave him was: "We are interrogating you, not vice versa." They produced a report that bore scant resemblance to what Huang had actually said during the interrogation, so he refused to sign it. But, to Huang's astonishment, an officer calmly

1 The Chinese term translated here as "evil cult" is used politically by Party officials to alienate and suppress various faith groups, including, for example, Protestant house churches. Former Party Chairman Jiang Zemin is said to have first used the term against Falun Gong when support for his persecution of the group was dwindling.

proceeded both to sign and fingerprint the report for him, right in front of him.

Huang later realized that the purpose of the report was to produce evidence in order to send him to a labor camp. On June 3, Huang was sentenced for the second time to three years in a labor camp. Thereafter, each time Huang wished to request that the city government review his case and the question of due process, he found that he had to go on a hunger strike before his request would be met. He fasted for a total of forty-two days.

On the morning of December 27, 2004, another lawyer and I arrived at the Shijiazhuang Labor Camp and followed the procedures to request a meeting with Huang Wei. The labor camp administration told us that they could approve requests to see any prisoner other than Falun Gong believers. They said we needed special approval from the 6-10 Office in order to see our client. In the end, three hours of red tape yielded a mere three-minute meeting with our client. We joked that we had been treated to three unlawful hours and three lawful minutes.

That afternoon, we took all the documents that composed Huang's complaint to the Shijiazhuang Intermediate Court. We tried filing the case, but to no avail. After having the complaint rejected again the next morning, one of the Intermediate Court's judges agreed to meet with us. The judge told us to take the case to the Xinhua District Court. Within an hour we were at the Xinhua District Court, where an administrative judge by the name of Miao examined the documents and said, "We have received orders from above indicating that, when it comes to Falun Gong, no case can be accepted and no document can be issued." When we pointed him to various legal provisions, he replied simply by saying that these were "orders from above" and that their job was only to follow them. He suggested we go to the case filing department.

At the case filing department, two female staff members grew irritated as they looked through our documents. As with Judge Miao, they told us that the court would not deal with any Falun Gong cases, adding that they had received documents from above. We responded by saying that the court should make its decisions about whether or not to accept cases based on Chinese law, and that documents that are in conflict with the law are invalid. At that point, one of the young staff members exploded, saying, "If you think the documents from above are invalid, you can ask the National People's Congress to amend the law."

As she finished, a judge who they called the "Presiding Judge" came in. The judge pointed at us and said, "You are probably not Party members, and you probably haven't studied the directives of the National Congress. Are you aware that lawyers aren't allowed to take cases like this? The court belongs to the Chinese Communist Party, and so do the laws. There are currently orders from above to reject these cases, and that's the end of it. Go talk to whoever you like and go file your case wherever you like. We don't care."

After formally inquiring with another judge, we were told to bring the case before the Chang'an District Court. We arrived at this third court, but as soon as we mentioned that the case involved Falun Gong, the judge handed the documents right back to us. The judge repeated the same story, adding that the orders from above stipulated that no documents justifying the court's decision to avoid these cases shall be produced. "What you lawyers are doing is very risky," the judge said. "If you continue, we'll need to deal with you by writing a judicial report demanding disciplinary action against you." Thus concluded our efforts to file a case in Shijiazhuang.

The above phenomena I came across while handling this case are at such odds with the rule of law that, as a lawyer, and as a Chinese person, I cannot remain silent.

The prison terms and fines imposed on Falun Gong people are in complete violation of basic legal principles and contemporary legal norms, for the following reasons:

1. Under any country's statutory law, the penal code dictates that laws cannot be applied ex post facto, that is, to behavior that occurred prior to the laws' enactment. But on October 30, 1999, the NPC Standing Committee promulgated the "Decision to Eradicate Evil Cult Organizations and to Prevent and Punish Evil Cult Activities" ("the Decision"). After this formality was put in place, the majority of criminal punishments citizens who practice Falun Gong received were aimed at their actions prior to the Decision's promulgation. That is, it is under the circumstance that our country's basic legal principles have been violated that they are being thrown into jail.

2. The penal code can only target people's actions, not their thoughts or group identity. Huang's case is only one example of how scores of citizens who practice Falun Gong have been punished simply because of their identity as Falun Gong adherents.

3. The Decision failed to provide any legal definitions for proper judgments regarding Falun Gong. It did not address, for instance: What is the relationship between the Falun Gong organization and "evil cult organizations"? What is an "evil cult organization"? In what ways do the

actions of Falun Gong adherents fall under the category of "evil cult" crimes? Falun Gong believers are accused basically across the board of "using an evil cult organization to undermine the implementation of the law." Yet there is a lack of evidence that any "evil cult organization" exists in this case.

4. The very existence of forced labor camps, and the way in which people are sentenced to them, clearly violates multiple articles of our constitution (such as Articles 5, 10, 33, 37, and 38). Forced labor deprives a citizen of his personal freedom, usually for years, yet there is no official channel for him to appeal the decision to relegate him to it. When he is notified of the decision to send him to a labor camp, he may be detained right on the spot and shipped off to the camp. This would be unimaginable in any civilized society. After a person is sent to a labor camp, every step of any "appeals" process requires painful means such as hunger strikes, perhaps for days, if one is to achieve anything. All citizens, including the police, know that the labor camp system violates the constitution and basic laws, but the system has continued, and the country is paying an increasingly high price for this.

5. The systematic and conniving way in which the national and local governments are handling the above-mentioned matters has brought about another consequence: Legal personnel are being encouraged to behave cruelly. With Huang's case, the irresponsibility of legal personnel and their corrupt, unprofessional conduct reached an alarming level. Most terrible of all is that they did not even see anything wrong with their behavior. Judges and courts of justice are the gatekeepers of legal values, and their professional code of ethics should instinctively alert them to deviations from these values. But with Huang's case, we have seen the exact opposite. These legal personnel attack anyone who attempts to uphold legal values. Although they are gatekeepers, they

haven't a trace of responsibility nor morality, and have no respect for the sacredness of their profession. This really pains me (and I believe Chairman Wu must feel the same as I do).

When I started writing this letter, people kindly warned me that Falun Gong is a politically sensitive issue. Being a lawyer, I am all too aware of China's current situation, and can say that, if power were wielded in a fair manner, what "sensitive issues" would there be to speak of? The fact that taboos exist demonstrates that power is being exercised in a distorted, unjust, and unscrupulous way. Why shouldn't citizens be allowed to comment on political issues? Whose politics is it if it cannot be discussed? Politics that can't be talked about must be unjust.

In recent years our country has made it a point to declare, internationally, that we are a responsible, great nation. To determine whether a nation is indeed responsible, one need look no further than the type of approval the government receives from its citizens. The fact that citizens are too terrified even to point out problems to the ruling authorities indicates how far removed we are from being a responsible, great nation.

In summary, my purpose in writing this letter to you, the NPC Standing Committee and its Chairman, is not to promote a certain group of people, nor to intentionally go against the Party or government. I love my country. And that is the only thing that inspires me these days. In addition, I am not writing this hoping merely to seek redress for Huang Wei. Rather, through eliciting the support of the NPC Standing Committee and Chairman Wu, I am hoping to systematically change the current distortion in legislation and law enforcement.

The nations in the world today whose governments do not adhere to the rule of law are closed, underdeveloped, unstable, and uncivilized. The citizens yearn for stability every bit as much as the government does. But the capricious use of the slogan, "maintaining stability is top priority," and thereby discarding the rule of law has become one of the greatest sources of instability in Chinese society today.

As far as Falun Gong practitioners are concerned, the authorities, especially legal personnel, should first recognize these people's status as Chinese citizens. Meanwhile, governmental and legal personnel must recognize that their professional role is one of representing the nation, and that they must follow the law in all their actions. If they overstep legal boundaries, who are they then representing? Even worse is that those violating the rules are precisely the law enforcement officials whose job it is to ensure their implementation. Over time they have come to see violating the law as routine practice and no longer think of upholding the country's law as a professional duty. Meanwhile, they undermine morality, legitimate use of power, and justice. Who does this ultimately serve? It serves only the ill-intended people who are holding members of our society hostage. We must guard against this with all our might!

I wish Chairman Wu good health.

Sincerely,

Gao Zhisheng
Shengzhi Law Office, Beijing

Open Letter to Chairman Hu Jintao and Premier Wen Jiabao

Stop Persecuting People of Faith and Make Amends With the Chinese People

October 18, 2005

Chairman Hu Jintao and Premier Wen Jiabao:

Greetings from a fellow Chinese citizen. Before being in a position to write to you, my compatriots, my concerns over another group of compatriots—Falun Gong believers—led me to travel to several places outside Beijing. I went to these places on a fact-finding investigation regarding a new wave of systematic, large-scale, organized, and illegal persecution that Falun Gong practitioners are being subjected to. During my days outside Beijing, I was in hiding, laying low like a thief. That is why some in the outside world were saying I was "missing."

This new round of barbarous persecution targeting our fellow Chinese citizens who believe in Falun Gong is an ongoing reality. This has not only been made clear to me through recent letters from different regions, but is also a fact those of us on the trip witnessed firsthand. As a citizen, and as a lawyer, I take full legal responsibility for the facts that I am publicizing.

Because I trust that you are men of goodwill, I decided to report to you in the form of an open letter what I have witnessed. I am putting my hope in you to take prompt measures to bring to a halt, in all regions, the authorities' continuing persecution of our Falun Gong compatriots. This is not only a matter of persecuted individuals needing to be freed from suffering; ending this persecution also involves the need to uphold China's constitution, the need for rule of law, and the need for the universal values of morality and justice. How could these things be considered worthless in China today? How could these things be worthless in your eyes?

On October 15, I met Xu Chengben of Wendeng city, Shandong province. As soon as he saw me, he said:

> "My wife He Xiuling's body has been kept frozen for almost two years. No one to date has been able to provide an explanation for her death, and that's why we can't go ahead and bury her. They went so far as to subject her to prolonged torture, eventually torturing her to death. But for almost two years, they haven't told us the cause of death.
>
> "I wasn't allowed to see her until she was tortured to the brink of death. When I got there, she had already lost consciousness. But even when she was in that condition, they cuffed her to a bed with her lower body completely naked. When I saw my loved one in such a tragic state, my heart broke! They are truly inhuman. I was only allowed to stay with her for a few minutes before they shoved me out of the room. She was only in her forties. That's what I witnessed the evening she passed away, after I had been notified by the police and rushed over to see her.
>
> "When she was alive, my wife was arrested five times. She was once held in Liaoning province for three months after filing a petition in Beijing on behalf of Falun Gong. She was held in the restroom of a hotel. The police rented the hotel specifically for the purpose of detaining Falun Gong practitioners. The restroom was only

about ten square feet large, but sixteen people were locked up in it. Many of them suffered greatly because they couldn't breathe.

"At our insistence, they performed an autopsy following her death, but to this day they haven't given me the report. After numerous requests, they merely told me verbally that 'she died because of practicing Falun Gong.'"

Falun Gong disciple Lin Jixiao from Shandong province was arrested on September 28, 2005, and locked up in a detention center. She went on a hunger strike in protest. When her family went to demand her release, they were told she had been sent to the Wangcun Labor Camp. But another person who had been released from the detention center said she was still at the first center and was dying. Her family then went to the Wangcun camp to check but was told that she was not there. They then went to ask the 6-10 Office officials, but were told she had been sent to Qingdao city. Is she still alive? Where on earth is she? It's still not clear.

Xiao Yong from Yantai city has always been a law-abiding citizen and very well regarded. But in July, he was sentenced to three-and-a-half years in prison just because he practiced Falun Gong.

A retired teacher, "Liu Li" (at her request, I am using a pseudonym), sat down and calmly told me the following:

"I was first arrested in June 2001. After just over a year of torture my health had deteriorated, so I was released. That was in 2003. When I got out, I found that the 6-10 Office had confiscated all of my wages since 2000. I talked to 6-10 Office staff and our school principal many times, but to no avail.

> "I went to the Fushan Town Communist Party Committee to ask the mayor, Mr. Che, about the illegal confiscation of my salary. I arrived at Mayor Che's office and, after I introduced myself, he stood up and walked out. I waited for a long time, and then he returned, saying: 'I'm going to have Secretary Zhao speak with you. Go to his office.' So I went to Mr. Zhao's office. As soon as I walked in the room, four or five policemen rushed in behind me, and dragged me into their car without any explanation. They took me to the Fushan Brainwashing Center, from which I wasn't released for another year.
>
> "When I was imprisoned, guards used utterly inhuman methods to torture me. I was handcuffed for forty-three days straight. With both my hands cuffed behind my back, I was hung over a metal door and beaten… Once I was denied sleep for twenty-six consecutive days. As soon as my eyes closed, they beat me awake. I fainted many times and they also made me stand continuously so I couldn't rest. They beat me to the point each time that they themselves were gasping for air."

On October 15, 2005, we met with Wang Dejiang, who is disabled. Even now, Wang's legs are still so swollen that he cannot wear any shoes. Wang told us:

> "On the evening of August 15, 2005, I was at a friend's house in Xiayu village. Suddenly, three people—from the village security team and the Gaoling Police Department—broke in, and my friend and I ran out. They yelled loudly: 'Catch the thieves!' The villagers were fooled and we were caught.

"The officers began to beat us. The man in charge picked up a chair and, in one strike, shattered it on my body. I lay on the ground and couldn't move. They continued to kick me. When one of them kicked my liver area I lost consciousness. Then they put me into a vehicle and drove me to the Gaoling Hospital emergency room. On waking up, I found that I was cuffed to a hospital bed. One of the police officers was particularly resentful, as he had tripped over me and fallen when they were trying to catch me before. So as soon as I woke up in the hospital, he beat me with the sole of his shoe. The other policemen said to him, 'You have to keep the noise down when you beat them in hospitals.'

"Later, I was sent to a detention center and coerced into registering for a brainwashing class. I tried to refuse, but the prison guards twisted my handcuffs hard, saying, 'Are you going to sign up or not?' I told them I wasn't going to. They kept twisting the handcuffs until they cut into my flesh…

"After being sent to a brainwashing class in Yantai against my will, I wasn't allowed to sleep and had to sit on a stool to undergo forced 'transformation.' They tried to make me write the 'three statements': a pledge letter (promising not to practice Falun Gong anymore), a statement denouncing Falun Gong, and a repentance statement. They took turns making me watch videos that slander Falun Gong.

"On the fourth day, they still couldn't get the results they wanted. I heard them saying that only the center in Zhaoyuan could handle people like me. By that point I had gone seven or eight days straight without food or sleep.

"As soon as we arrived in Zhaoyuan, guards lifted me up and started kicking me as they dragged me into the complex—one kick per step as they walked. They said, 'Let's see if you don't transform.' After they put me down, I no longer had the strength to stand up and just lay on the ground.

"The director of the center started stomping on my genitals with his foot. His face was completely expressionless as he was doing this. He also lifted my head with his foot and then quickly removed it, making my head smash against the ground; he repeated this over and over. Only when they were done torturing me did they put me in a prison cell. I felt that they lacked even a trace of humanity.

"Each Falun Gong practitioner at Zhaoyuan was locked in a separate, small room designed specifically for brainwashing. They used a chain to bind me to a metal chair, cuffed my hands and shackled my feet. I still refused to transform.

"On the tenth day they started to force-feed me. I began constantly vomiting blood. When that happened, even they couldn't bear the sight of it and started to vomit as well. The director asked me if I would give up my practice. I responded, 'no.' He said, 'Don't even think about getting out of Zhaoyuan without transforming. We have plenty of ways to deal with you.

"They hung me from a heating pipe with only the tips of my toes touching the ground. There was no light in the cell, so it was dark twenty-four hours a day. I had a vague sense that someone kept coming into the cell and putting his hand under my nose to see if I was still breathing, but I had no idea how much time passed. My

> wrists had big cuts in them from the tight strap, and my mouth was bound shut with wire. Even now I can't help drooling when I speak.
>
> "Being constantly tortured, I was in such pain that it's beyond description, and I even thought about killing myself. I wanted to swallow my tongue, but they put a few more wires in my mouth, making me unable to move it. Eventually I lost consciousness.
>
> "When I came to, I saw that my legs had started to turn black. My left leg swelled up more and more, until it was twice as wide as my right leg, which was getting thinner and thinner. But they still wouldn't let up in torturing me. When I wanted to go to the restroom, they lifted me from under my arms, but I discovered I could no longer walk and fell to the floor. Then they lifted me onto a bed, keeping my right leg tied and both hands cuffed.
>
> "The doctor there found out my health was so poor and asked them to put me in the hospital. After I was transferred to the hospital, the doctor said my life was in danger and that my legs had to be amputated. So they sent me to Yuhuangding Hospital, which was supposed to have the best medical equipment. I was there for a few days. They asked my family to pay for my treatment, but we had no money, so my family took me home. Once I was back home, since I could no longer take care of myself, I had to be looked after by my 80-year-old mother."

Who knows how many innocent fellow citizens throughout the country are still experiencing nightmares like this?

> "Yang Kemeng was in his second year at Harbin Institute of Technology, where he was studying Automobile Engineering. Everyone liked him, from his classmates to the university president. But because he publicly announced his withdrawal from the Chinese Communist Youth League (CCYL), he was singled out by a central government official, who issued an order to track him down. Since Yang didn't identify his school in his statement of withdrawal from the CCYL, the 6-10 Office launched a thorough investigation involving all of the institutions of higher education throughout the country. In May 2005, 6-10 Office staff found Yang and asked him if he practiced Falun Gong and whether he had announced his withdrawal from the CCYL on the Internet. Yang replied, 'I may withdraw as I wish.' When the new school year started in August, the 6-10 Office staff returned and took him away. His parents didn't know a thing about it until they called his dorm. Then on September 7, Mr. Yang's parents and three others were simultaneously arrested. Their whereabouts are unknown."

A teacher named Wang related the above story to us.

> "Ahead of the October 1, 2005 National Day, major officials in Shandong province gave notice to the Laiwu City Police Department, stating that if they couldn't capture seven specific Falun Gong practitioners, all the high-ranking officers in the police department would be removed. At 1 A.M. on September 29, the seven people were arrested. The truth is, many police officers are unwilling to search for and arrest Falun Gong practitioners, but they have no choice.

"People from all over the country have traveled to the Zhaoyuan Brainwashing Center to learn from the staff there about how to administer the worst sorts of torture. While Hu Jintao was visiting the U.S., the Party's Central Committee issued an order calling for a concerted effort to reform those who were not working hard enough in persecuting Falun Gong. These people were told to intensify their suppression efforts. The Central Committee pointed to the Zhaoyuan Brainwashing Center in Shandong province and another in Shanxi as models. Those outside the camps have no idea what goes on in there… hardly anyone can survive these places. They make hell seem like nothing. The people torturing us have turned into monsters."

That was relayed to us by a believer who had been locked up at the Zhaoyuan Brainwashing Center.

"My name is Qi Xin. I'm nineteen years old and from Laiwu city in Shandong province… My parents started to practice Falun Gong in 1998. In 2000, while my dad was doing the Falun Gong exercises in a park, police kidnapped him and he was later sentenced to three years in Wangcun Labor Camp. My mom left home to avoid the police but was later caught and detained. I was thirteen years old and my brother was only three, so I had to look after him on my own as we waited for my mom's return.

"After his release, my dad told me that to try make him give up his self-cultivation practice, guards at the forced labor camp had shocked him with eight electric batons, simultaneously. He was on the floor and his body couldn't stop trembling, and his skin emitted a burnt smell. Several weeks after the electric shocks, his scorched skin began to slough off layer by layer.

> "Later on, after both my parents came home, our family started to live together again. They re-opened their store, and we thought that our ordeal was over. But at 1 A.M. on September 30, over twenty armed police entered my aunt's home in Wenyang village and kidnapped her, her husband, and my parents.
>
> "Since my parents knew the police were after them, they had left me with another auntie in August, a month before the incident. They themselves began wandering around with my brother like homeless people. Our family has again been forced apart. I've received no news of my brother since their abduction. I'm so worried about my little innocent brother and pray for him every day."

Late one September evening, several policemen suddenly burst into the Guangzhou home of a man named Shi Lei. Without any explanation, they grabbed him and ran. "My husband didn't even have time to put on his shoes before they took him. As soon as they went downstairs with him and got into their police van, they started beating him. When I heard the sound of the beating, I felt as if a knife was piercing my heart. Mr. Gao, we feel totally helpless," his sobbing wife told me over the phone.

Mr. Hu and Mr. Wen, some local government authorities have been persecuting Falun Gong believers, our fellow countrymen, such that these officials use whatever methods they so choose. We are living in the twenty-first century, and in a country that is supposedly ruled by a government. We simply cannot condone such brazenly inhumane, savage acts.

The two of you, as with all of us, must face the following reality: When you first rose to your current positions, people both inside and outside China expected great things of you. The principles you have been promoting, such as "governing the country according to the constitution," "putting the people first," and "building a harmonious society" have, for a long time, raised people's hopes.

The fact of the matter, however, is stark and real. It is a reality that the citizens being persecuted have had to face, and is something that you, and all of us, need to face as well. Since you are the leaders of such a major country, we of course are unwilling to believe or accept the idea that you might know less about this matter than the average citizen. If you have no knowledge of the atrocities being committed openly against the innocent Falun Gong practitioners, something even children are aware of, then your ignorance is itself a crime. If, on the other hand, you are aware of the situation but are doing nothing to stop it, then how are you any different from those committing the acts of violence?

I write this open letter to you because I still have faith in you. I have found during my investigations that many of the Falun Gong practitioners who have been disabled, or even lost loved ones, feel similarly. These people's compassion and high hopes for you have brought tears to my eyes.

Meanwhile, we must face the fact that in this disastrous persecution of Falun Gong practitioners, evil reigns. This unremitting, inhuman evil has not only brought tragedy to countless men and women who practice Falun Gong—many of whom have lost their lives—but has also tarnished the image of our government and our nation. The damage will continue as long as the persecution does.

This catastrophe didn't start with you, but it has continued under your watch. And since you have not acted to stop the tragedy that these people of faith face, you are liable for these crimes. If you do not end it right away, eventually you will see that history condemns, as I have, what has taken place, and it will no longer be a matter of simply one person's opinion.

The incessant tragedies that this particular group has been subjected to have harmed not only the victims and their families, but also the persecutors themselves. I am struck with utter grief on seeing how the perpetrators have lost every last trace of humanity.

Since those who carry out the "transformation" of Falun Gong believers are evaluated by their supervisors solely based on the results they produce, they are driven by financial gain to the point where they have lost any normal human sense of sympathy, fear, guilt, shame, or morality.

For generations to come, people will recall with rage the unimaginable agony He Xiuling was put through before her ultimate death. While just barely hanging on to life, she was pronounced dead and sent to the mortuary. Her family members, who had been barred from visiting her up until that point, knelt in front of her dying body. Grieving over the loss, they began to enumerate the awful experiences she had when suddenly they noticed tears welling up in her "dead" eyes. They screamed and cried and did everything they possibly could to get a doctor to come, but the doctors remained aloof. One of the doctors' indifference softened only when a villager that he knew came along, as he was planning on attending the funeral. When that doctor found out the woman's heart was still beating, his first reaction was not to save her, but to rip out the electrocardiogram. "She died ages ago. Alive? What are you talking about?" the doctor said, and then fled. He Xiuling died with tears in her eyes and to the sound of her family wailing in despair.

My two compatriots, I don't know what goes through your mind as you read this. Our nation, our people, the values that we have inherited from antiquity, and the moral standing of all the world's governments that have remained shamefully reticent in the face of this great calamity—all of these have fallen victim to this catastrophe.

The reality we are facing tells us that our leaders have failed to recognize the changes that have taken place in our society spiritually as a result of the tremendous economic growth. This being a time of peace for our country, and one in which the economy is flourishing, it is to be expected that there will come a time when people can no longer content themselves with indulging in material things alone. People's growing need for spirituality will naturally engender a large-scale, grassroots resurgence of religious and spiritual beliefs.

Spiritual pursuit, just as with more prevalent interests such as science and culture, is an integral part of society. These things are not mutually exclusive. Modern civilization has long since recognized that science and religion each serve a purpose, and that one should not supersede the other. Meanwhile, it is also true that individual freedom of belief results in the disintegration of any collective ideology, and that the expansion of individual rights likewise diminishes a government's absolute authority. This is the historical trend, and it is something rulers must be able to recognize and adapt to.

Here I must add that I am very confused about the cause and motivation behind this persecution, as are many of my colleagues, neighbors, and friends. Why should a citizen's freely chosen belief system, which cares not for worldly pursuits, become the basis for such lasting, inhumane, and illegal oppression? What is the purpose? The only explanation I have been able to come to is that those behind this persecution have lost their minds and are devoid of humanity. Their vileness sends a chill down the spine.

Other than demonstrating that this persecution continues, our investigation also revealed that this persecution has failed. What we observed in the different regions we visited was that the crueler the oppression was, the more prominent were the signs of its failure, and the more thorough was the extent of the failure.

For instance, in three cities in Shandong province—Jinan, Qingdao, and Yantai—posters and flyers exposing the persecution of Falun Gong are ubiquitous; they can even be spotted right in front of many police stations. Tenacious and enduring resistance is spreading and intensifying, thus indicating how unpopular this persecution policy has become. Conversely, where the persecution is not as intense, a different scene manifests and the overall situation is relatively calm.

Immeasurable capital and police resources are being poured into this campaign for no reason, turning society into chaos, all just to suppress Falun Gong practitioners—people who peacefully do their practice in order to cultivate their hearts and minds, and improve their health. What is being done to them is an absolute crime and a violation of basic human rights. There is no excuse for you not to take immediate action to change the situation.

China is a signatory to the Universal Declaration of Human Rights, which explicitly states: "Everyone has the right to life, liberty and security of person"; "No one shall be subjected to arbitrary arrest, detention or exile"; "Everyone has the right to an effective remedy by the competent national tribunals for acts violating the fundamental rights granted him by the constitution or by law."

Article 33 of our own constitution also declares, "The State respects and preserves human rights."

From the perspective of international law and norms or of our constitution, it is absolutely unacceptable for anyone to persecute or violate the rights of a fellow citizen. And it is precisely out of my belief in mankind's universal values and respect for rule of law that I solemnly suggest that both of you make your minds up as soon as possible to stop persecuting people of faith, make amends with the Chinese people, and earnestly put into action a plan to rule according to the constitution. With democracy, rule of law, and constitutionalism as a foundation, you can create a new China.

If you do this, the Chinese people and the people of the world will give you limitless support!

Finally, I must specifically state that you should guarantee that all the citizens mentioned here, people who have already suffered tremendously, will not be subjected to further savage persecution as a result of this open letter. It is because of previous experience that I must remind you of this. Falun Gong practitioner Hao Qiuyan of Shijiazhuang city was jailed for eight months because I mentioned her case in a open letter. With whatever days of freedom I have left, I will continue to monitor closely these people's safety. Be it as a member of the human race, as a

Chinese person, as a Chinese citizen, or as a lawyer, it is my right to do so, even though doing so in China is extremely dangerous.

I wish you both peace, safety, and success.

Your fellow Chinese citizen,

Gao Zhisheng

Second Open Letter to Chairman Hu and Premier Wen

A Citizen Asks You to Address Several Questions

November 22, 2005

To our nation's leaders, Hu Jintao and Wen Jiabao:

Ever since the morning of October 20, 2005, approximately twenty plainclothes officers from the Beijing Public Security Bureau and the Beijing Police Department have been closely monitoring my family and me. The entrance to my home is surrounded by at least nine vehicles every day. On October 18, 19, and 20, over twenty vehicles were parked outside my home. Since you are our nation's leaders, I sincerely hope you will answer the following questions:

1. Did you tell those tired young faces who monitor me day and night the truth about what I, Gao Zhisheng, have done? Or is it that you deceived them?

2. Did you inform those young people about how treating innocent citizens this way violates China's constitution and China's basic legal principles? Have you told them this is illegal?

3. Have you told that group of young people that treating innocent people this way is absolutely despicable and immoral?

4. Have you told that group of young people—who are also innocent—shivering at night outside our doorway that the way you manage to curb my entire family's personal freedom, threaten, and terrorize

us, is by using the most dishonorable, uncivil, and base means in the world today?

5. Have you explained to that group of young people the purpose of closely monitoring my family around the clock?

6. Have you told those young people that the Chinese people gnash their teeth at the tactics they are using, and that in the eyes of the absolute majority of Chinese this behavior is most disgraceful?

These past couple of mornings I did not go out to get my morning exercise because I could not bear to trouble the nearly twenty young plainclothes officers guarding my front door. To tell you the truth, when I lie in bed at night I feel very uneasy as I think of those young police officers. They too have families—parents, spouses, and children—and should have the right and opportunity to spend these cold nights comfortably at home with them. Whenever my wife and I look outside our window in the early morning after waking up, and see them bouncing up and down to stay warm, our hearts are pained. This morning, my wife and I tried to figure out a way to get them hot water to drink. These people are my beloved fellow citizens; they are surely not my enemies. Whenever I see that they are unwilling even to look at me, I grieve inside. I sense their kindness, as well as their guilty consciences. I must clarify, however, that although I have sympathy for them, I have not an ounce of respect!

Gentlemen, people in a civilized country would find it absurd to see a citizen who, having had his or her legal rights encroached upon, decided to take recourse by writing directly to the national leaders. But in our country, this is the only recourse left for me at present.

On October 18, 2005, I expressed my sorrow to both of you through an open letter. I exposed what has been happening to those citizens who assert their freedom of belief. Local authorities are flouting our nation's laws and cruelly persecuting these people. My intention was to relay this information so that this impediment to China's development could be promptly addressed and harmony could prevail throughout the country. This would require a joint effort on your part and on the part of the Chinese people. But I am upset and disheartened to see that your response to my suggestions goes in the opposite direction.

The day after I made my letter public, I received phone calls threatening my family and me. The next day, my wife was shocked to learn that two strangers had been following my twelve-year-old daughter to and from school. Then, starting on November 15, they began following me instead. Since November 20, at least three officers have been taking turns monitoring the entrances to my house and law firm. The day after these people arrived, my wife's bicycle mysteriously disappeared, and last night, under the watchful eye of over twenty police officers, two valves were removed from our new bicycle and graffiti was put on my car.

The Beijing Judicial Bureau then suspended my law firm's license for a year. That was November 4. When I left for Xinjiang province on November 15 to attend a court session, the same policemen who had followed my daughter followed me until I boarded my flight. Local officers then monitored me after I landed. What I find most inconceivable is that officials from the Ministry of Justice contacted government departments in Xinjiang to have them investigate my family background and political beliefs, to look into whether I have a criminal or disciplinary record, to find out how I managed to become a lawyer, and to determine how it is that I went from being a lawyer to being a "bad element." They are employing the same contemptible tactics once used during the Cultural Revolution, and I don't know whether to laugh or cry.

As soon as I returned to Beijing the day before yesterday, two friends of mine from the United Nations arrived in Beijing—Ms. Kong Shan and the United Nations Special Rapporteur on Torture, Mr. Manfred Nowak. On my way to visit them at a hotel, an officer side-swiped my car at fifty miles per hour, which shocked the representative of Mr. Nowak who was with me.

During the dinner with my foreign friends we took a group picture. But it turned out that one of the plainclothes policeman who was following us ended up in the photo. He protested, saying our photographing him "severely violated his human rights."

These people's rude and abusive behavior shocked the U.N. human rights experts. The customers on that floor of the restaurant surrounded us to catch a glimpse of the shenanigans. The plainclothes officers were out of control, pointing their fingers and stomping their feet while howling. They became so worked up that Ms. Kong Shan was forced to delete the photo. The human rights officers simply shook their heads. We quickly finished our dinner and left with a few policemen closely behind us.

During those two days, my neighborhood was overwhelmed by at least twenty vehicles that surrounded my residence. Ever since I returned home on November 20, my home has become a police hangout. They also disconnected my home telephone, and as of now we still can't use it.

People in my neighborhood who know me well do not understand the government's insane behavior. Last night, after I parked my car, my wife looked out our window and saw seven or eight officers searching around my car for over an hour. Nobody could figure out what they were up to. At midnight, they kept creeping around our apartment entrance. I couldn't sleep because of the patter of footsteps. Do they really think my family spends our nights secretly plotting how to undermine national security?

Now that I am writing to you both, I would like to ask a question on behalf of my children: Why do you allow this political game to continue? I don't believe that every one of the young officers has a dark heart, but I do believe that the commanding officer who instigated this must be rotten to the core.

Our children, and each of us, have the right to respectfully ask you both: Who is actually giving the orders to do such wicked things? Our country is still far from being wealthy. We have 900 million peasants living in poverty. Because of poverty, there are tens of millions of children who cannot afford to go to school or have to drop out. Instead of being used to help them, taxpayers' hard-earned money is being spent on tormenting those unfortunate plainclothes police and on the despicable process of persecuting the country's own citizens. With such underhanded, low actions taking place, I don't know how you can put on suits and face the civilized world or your own citizens.

While writing this letter, I received a phone call from a professor in the northeast. He believes that it is not you who ordered this foul thing, and I agree. The crux of the matter, however, is that under your administration such ignoble acts can happen anytime, anywhere, and to anyone. Please don't think today's Chinese people are not intelligent enough to realize this. China's current problems can continue no further! Suppressing me, Gao Zhisheng, is of no consequence, but to continue going against the law of Heaven with such tyranny is to ultimately meet with destruction.

Until this illegal and despicable persecution of my family concludes, I am going to do two things. First, every day, through the form of a public statement, I will urge your government to observe China's laws. Second, I will prepare to sue the two units that are illegally persecuting my family.

Again, I wish you both peace, safety, and success.

Gao Zhisheng

Open Letter to Chairman Hu, Premier Wen, and My Fellow Chinese

The Atrocities Corrupting Our National Conscience Must Immediately Cease

December 12, 2005

Hu Jintao, Wen Jiabao, and all other conscientious fellow Chinese:

Greetings from Changchun city. I would first like to express my deepest grief over the killing of our Chinese compatriots at the hands of the Guangdong province government,[2] and offer my condolences to the innocent victims' families. At the same time, I would like to register my strongest protest against this slaughter of our good countrymen. I exhort our highest authorities to follow the norm of civilized societies by punishing those responsible for the murders and comforting and compensating the victims' families.

Winter in Changchun is extremely cold, and although I am in hiding in a room that has no running water most of the time, my blood is boiling. I feel this way not because I am again writing an open letter to you; rather, it is the passion of working for the future of one of the greatest nations in the world.

On October 18, also with much passion, I wrote an open letter to you, urgently calling on your government to stop persecuting people of faith. The very next day, I received threatening phone calls at my home. From the third day on, at least ten vehicles and twenty plainclothes

2 A reference to the Shanwei Massacre. See chapter three.

police officers have been hovering around, monitoring, and following my entire family twenty-four hours a day. Fifteen days after I wrote the letter, the Beijing Judicial Bureau illegally shut down my law firm.

Yet my letter also triggered a strong response from Falun Gong believers in various parts of China, who began writing to invite me to their areas so I might learn more about how they have been persecuted. So, starting on November 29, I began traveling around the clock among major cities in Shandong, Liaoning, and Jilin provinces. Unlike my usual practice of traveling solo, this time I was honored to have the company of Professor Jiao Guobiao.[3]

As flocks of plainclothes police hovered around my house, terrorizing my family, I managed to escape and spend fifteen days investigating the truth in my own way. It is time for our nation and each and every one of us to face our problems with all due seriousness. Any excuse or delay amounts to betraying our country!

In this letter, I will not circumvent any of the real problems I saw, even if this means I am arrested as soon as this letter is made public. The fifteen days of investigation showed me yet another painful truth. Within the realm of the nation's political power exists a gestapo-like organization that is able to make use of all the regime's resources. It is known as the 6-10 Office. This entity has powers that no civilized state in the world would even consider trying to obtain.

This organization is continuously tormenting our mothers, sisters, children, and our entire nation. Since you are citizens of our nation who currently hold special positions, and especially since you are people

---

3 Jiao was a leading professor of journalism at China's prestigious Peking University until his recent dismissal for public criticism of the Party's media censorship.

whom the majority of the public perceives as conscientious, the time has arrived, Mr. Hu and Mr. Wen, for you to confront this problem with us!

With a trembling heart and a trembling pen, I record the tragic experiences of those who have been persecuted in the last six years. Of all the true accounts of incredible violence that I have heard, of all the records of the government's inhuman torture of its own people, what has shaken me most is the routine practice on the part of the 6-10 Office and the police of assaulting women's genitals. Of those persecuted, almost every man's and woman's genitals and every woman's breasts have been assaulted in a most vulgar fashion. Almost all who have been persecuted, be they male or female, were stripped naked before being tortured. No words can describe our government's vulgarity and immorality. Who, that can rightly be called a human being, could possibly stay silent in the face of these facts?

The experiences above were relayed to me by a woman who spoke so rapidly she almost told the entire story in one breath.

> "At 4:20 P.M. on October 28, 2005, Ms. Wang Shouhui and Mr. Liu Boyang, mother and son, were followed by Changchun city's 6-10 Office personnel and illegally arrested. The two were brutally tortured by the police. By about 8 P.M., Liu Boyang, who was only twenty-eight, was dead. About ten days later, his mother was also tortured to death. The bodies of the unfortunate pair are still in the hands of the 6-10 Office. Liu's father scoured the city for a lawyer, but no one would dare take his case. He said, 'In this kind of society, it's harder to live than to die. Living brings more pain. After I take care of their burials, I'll follow them and leave, too.'

"Wang Shouhui, her husband, and her son Liu Boyang began practicing Falun Gong in 1995. Police and officials harassed them ever since the persecution of Falun Gong was launched on July 20, 1999. Ms. Wang was illegally detained in October 1999 and sent to the Heizuizi Labor Camp the following February. There she was tortured with an electric baton eight times. She was forced to work during the day, and to remain standing, disallowed to sleep, for five days straight. Once, she was assaulted with two electric batons for over an hour while tied to the 'death bed' torture rack. Not a single part of her body or face remained intact, and she was only released after the torture put her life in grave danger.

"On April 11, 2002, Ms. Wang was walking down the street when policemen again abducted her. She was blindfolded and taken to a secret torture chamber in the Jingyue Mountains, near Changchun. There she was tormented on the 'tiger bench' torture rack for two days and one night, during which time two electric batons were used simultaneously to shock her breasts. Three men punched her in the face, chest, and back. Her cheekbone cracked and she vomited a great amount of blood. Later, her lungs became inflamed.

"After she was released, on June 27, 2002, policemen again abducted Ms. Wang and her family. Guards handcuffed her arms to her ankle shackles for eighteen days and force-fed her for a month.

"All the while, several officers from the Zhengyang Police Station tortured, beat, and kicked her son, Liu Boyang. They hit him in the face with their leather shoes, tied him up with rope, covered his head with a plastic bag, tied his arms behind his back, and

> hung him from the ceiling with handcuffs. As he hung there, they pulled and swung his legs. Yuan Dachuan, one of the police officers carrying out the torture, told him, 'I've tortured quite a few Falun Gong practitioners to death. And I won't be held accountable if I beat you to death.' Whenever they were tortured, the mother and son could hear each other's screams.
>
> "Liu was a medical doctor. He was a good person—kind to children and respectful of the elderly. Every year the hospital named him a model worker."

Sun Shuxiang, a forty-eight-year-old Changchun resident, was illegally arrested nine times in six years. Below are some of the experiences she described:

> "In July 2002, I was in my father's home. A plainclothes policeman suddenly broke in and asked if I was Sun Shuxiang. Before I had a chance to answer, they abducted me. The next day, policemen put me in a car and drove me on a rough road for about two hours. Two policemen led me to a dark, terrifying basement, and removed the blindfolds. Eight or nine policemen quickly moved into the room. On a table were three electric batons of large, medium, and small sizes and a bundle of rope. Across the way were three tiger benches. Two policemen forced me on a tiger bench, and placed my hands on the armrests. My hands were then locked in place with handcuffs connected to the armrests; there were sets of different size cuffs for different size wrists. The police dexterously fixed an iron rod to the two armrests, pressing it against my chest and abdomen area, which made it impossible for me to move.

"One policeman pointed at the torture devices and said to me, 'Do you see that? If you cooperate, we can finish business in about an hour. Otherwise, we'll give you a taste of all kinds of devices. What happened to Liu Zhe and the others, people wonder? Only a few come out of here alive.'

"A policeman who seemed to have a gentle expression slapped my face twice and asked if I knew any other Falun Gong practitioners. I said I didn't. He grabbed an electric baton, jabbed its two electrodes between my ribs, and started shocking me. He asked for my fellow practitioners' phone numbers, and I said nothing. He then used the electric baton on my fingertips while again asking me which practitioners I knew. He used the electric baton on one of my arms and my head, and then on the other arm and the other side of my body. After one round of covering my body, he slowly shocked the different parts of my body again. Then they switched to a higher voltage electric baton, and shocked my whole body, from my toes on up. I continued to stay silent. Starting with my other foot's toes they shocked my body again going in the opposite direction. I was still silent. Then they used the electric baton on my eyes. I felt like my eyes were about to pop out of their sockets, and I couldn't see anything. But I still refused to speak, and they went back to shocking my ribs. The pain was unbearable. The electric baton moved to my chest, as they asked me with which practitioners I had remained in contact. The pain made it impossible for me to speak, and the familiar faces of practitioners flashed before my eyes. I had only one thought: 'No matter what, I'm not going to expose anyone, because as soon as I do, that person will be arrested and tortured.' The police stuck the electric baton in my mouth, and my mouth became all burnt and swollen, with blisters covering the lips. As they were shocking me, they said, 'If you don't talk, we'll pry open your mouth.' They again stuck the electric baton inside my mouth. After a day and night of torture, I was on the brink of death...

"In the beginning of 2003, I was temporarily staying at a Ms. Xing Guiling's house when in the middle of the night I heard a loud pounding on the door. Her two doors were suddenly broken through and I was terrified, as in front of me were a bunch of policemen with hammers and guns, shouting, 'Don't move or you're dead.' We were arrested and locked up in a small metal cage. I was tied to a tiger bench. They started to beat Ms. Xing in front of me, wrapping a leather belt around her neck and pulling it tightly. She screamed hysterically, as if her lungs were splitting. Then I saw her beaten down to the ground. When she was down, they kicked her. When she got up, they beat her down again. They beat and kicked her, demanding that she tell them which practitioners she knew. The policemen shouted, 'This is what you get for not talking.' She was tortured until she was on her last breath, but she still wouldn't reveal a single person's name. Then they started to torture me. After three days and nights of torture, they sent us to the No. 3 Detention Center.

"That August I was arrested again. When I was in custody, a policeman with moles on his face grabbed me by the hair and kept bashing my head against the wall... Then he forced me onto a tiger bench and cuffed my wrists tightly. Another policeman started to hit my arms, and my wrists began to bleed. They put my ankles in shackles, and then stepped on the shackles to make them tighter and tighter. The pain in my ankles was unbearable. Then they covered my head with a plastic bag and tied it around my neck. When they saw that I was about to suffocate to death they took off the bag. After a while, they covered my head again and then took it off again just before I would have died. The pain was so great that I had a seizure. The skin on my ankles was broken and I was bleeding a lot. I fainted. They used cold water to revive me, and sent me to a detention center."

Liu Shuqin, a sixty-year-old woman from Changchun calmly told us the barbarous torture she suffered:

"On December 31, 2000, I was arrested for the second time when I went to Beijing to petition the government. I held up a banner that said 'Falun Dafa[4] is Good,' and the Tiananmen Square police officers hit my back with electric batons and forced me into a police car. Later I was thrown into a dungeon whose walls were covered with ice. They forced me to take off all my clothing, and sprayed me with water from a big hose. Then they left me naked on the bare floor. They subjected me to sleep deprivation and interrogated me for thirty-eight days, but they didn't get a thing out of me.

"On February 28, 2003, a group of policemen from Luyuan Police Station broke into my home again. They raided my home, confiscated all five hundred dollars I had without issuing any receipt, and abducted me. They took me to the torture chamber at Luyuan Police Station. As soon as we arrived at the torture chamber, they forced me onto a tiger bench, and about six policemen handcuffed me and chained my ankles, fixing a steel rod across my chest. A young policeman used a foot-long metal rod to hit my left hand, which was cuffed to the tiger bench. After a dozen

4 Another name for Falun Gong.

strikes, my hand was severely swollen and turned purplish-black. They asked me to disclose other practitioners' names, but I told them I wasn't going to say anything… I was tortured like this for a day and a night, falling in and out of consciousness. Police pulled the handcuffs and ankle chains to tighten them. My wrists and ankles were a mix of blood and raw flesh, and the wounds created a large pool of blood on the floor.

"That is how the police treated an old lady like me… Every nerve and bone in my arms, hands, feet, and legs was in agony. Eventually I couldn't move at all… I was diagnosed with a stroke and atrophy. I was originally very healthy, but that year of persecution put me into this state. Simply for wanting to be a good person I was subjected to torture like that for such a long time."

In a slow and gentle voice, Zhang Zhikui calmly told us what he had been through:

"After Falun Gong was banned on July 20, 1999, I went to Beijing to petition the government. Because I clarified the truth about Falun Gong to Beijing residents, I was arrested. They tied my hands and feet together around a wooden pole and hung me by putting the ends of the pole on two tables. I swung back and forth. Then the pole broke and I fell to the floor…

"On National Day in 2000, I was arrested for unfurling a banner in Changchun. Since all the news media in China have been lying, and they haven't said even one factual thing in our defense, I decided to use that method to let people know the truth.

"After I was arrested, Police Chief Liang and other police officers ripped my coat off and put it over my head. They cuffed my hands behind my back, dragged me down a flight of stairs, and escorted me to a car. After being on the road for about two hours I was taken to a house and the coat was removed. It was an awful place. There was a tiger bench in the room. I could sense that we were on a mountain and could hear the wind howling. Liang and the others stripped me naked and forced me onto the tiger bench. They placed iron rods over my chest, thighs, and legs… Then Liang took out a big, sharp knife and wiped the blade across his pant leg a couple of times. He then threw the knife to the table and said fiercely, 'Zhang Zhikui, you're going to die here. I'm going to torture you to death today and dig a hole and bury you. Nobody's going to know and nobody's going to find you.'

"After saying that, he walked out. The police officers started recharging the electric batons. Two of the police grabbed my hands, which were tied to a rod behind me, and lifted my arms up over my head from back to front. I heard my bones cracking one by one. They repeated this a few times and the pain was overwhelming. Later, they put a metal bucket over my head and banged the bucket with pipes. My head felt like it was exploding. The policemen then burned my back with cigarette butts and the pain was so unbearable that I lost consciousness. So they poured cold water on me to make me come to. Then they lit candles and used them to burn my back. After they scorched the flesh on my back, they poured hot wax on it. The pain made my body writhe and jolt to no end. Because in the end they couldn't find a single normal piece of skin left, they started shocking my penis with electric batons and piercing through it with something Then they smashed the end of my penis with a metal rod and I passed out.

"After one night of torture, my face had swollen to several times its normal size and my body was drenched in blood. I looked badly mangled. I had contorted my body so much because of the pain that the flesh around my ankles was cut through to the bone. When they saw that I had come to, they dragged me outside. It was under fourteen degrees Fahrenheit and they poured cold water over my naked body. They went back inside the house and left me lying there. Half an hour later they came out to check if I was still alive. I don't know how much time passed before morning arrived. I was near death.

"I was carried to the Changchun city police station. There were many small cells inside, each with a tiger bench in it. On each tiger bench was a female Falun Gong practitioner. Most of them were unconscious, with their lower bodies naked or with only a cloth covering them…

"At that police station, if a Falun Gong practitioner made even a little sound while sleeping, the other prisoners would beat him up. This frightened us out of sleeping. I sometimes couldn't stop coughing at night, and so the prisoners beat me all night… Once, I couldn't help but go to the restroom, and I went quietly. When I came back, someone named Xu Hui beat me up until I was almost dead. He kicked me with all his might in the area of my kidney, knocking it out of its natural position. I couldn't move for several days.

"One time, the other prisoners discovered that a Falun Gong practitioner in his twenties had hidden in his clothing teachings written by Falun Gong's founder, so they pounded him with a wrench over fifty times. He died shortly after. My younger sister

> was sentenced to ten years in prison and her husband to three. Just because they practiced Falun Gong, their nine-year-old child was expelled from school under orders from the 6-10 Office. Of the Falun Gong practitioners I've kept in touch with, eight or nine have been beaten to death.
>
> "When police tried to arrest my younger sister, she jumped from her building and her ribs broke, puncturing her organs. Her legs and arms broke, too, and she fainted. Passersby stopped to look at her and asked what had happened. One of the 6-10 policemen who was there said, 'She had a fight with her husband over a divorce.' Since they considered her an important Falun Gong practitioner, one who they would want to interrogate, the police took her to the hospital. But the doctors thought it wasn't necessary to try rescuing a Falun Gong practitioner. They said, 'Just throw her out,' and surprisingly, the police did leave her out in some suburban area. Later, some kind people saved her life. So the police put her back on the wanted list."

Wang Yuhuan is a Falun Gong believer who was arrested in Changchun and has been in and out of jails and labor camps a total of nine times. She recalled the following:

> "...They tied me up with rope and put me in the trunk of a police car. They drove to a mountain... Many of my fellow practitioners, such as Mr. Liu Haibo, have been tortured to death in that place. He had been stripped naked and forced to kneel. Police inserted the longest electric baton they could find into his anus and gave him internal electric shocks. He died on the spot.

"Twenty-three practitioners were tortured to death there. I knew many of them. The police simply buried their bodies in a pit. After Xiang Min, a nice-looking woman, came back from being tortured, she told me that the policemen assaulted her by groping and electrocuting her at the same time.

"It took over two hours for them to drive me to that devil's den in a mountain. I heard them stop the car… They dragged me along and banged me against trees as they took me to a building… One of the police said, 'Let's wait and see how you die today. Nobody has come out of here alive!'… There was a bed in the room for the police to rest on when they grew weary from torturing us. I saw a tiger bench and many policemen busily preparing to torture me. The wind was blowing angrily outside.

"A few policemen forced me onto the tiger bench… They started a round of torture every five minutes. They wrenched my arms back and forth, and I could hear my bones cracking. The terrible pain made me almost faint. They shoved my head down toward my legs and my whole body started to shake. Because my body had been bound to the tiger bench, I felt my neck cracking and the metal rods pressing hard against my breasts and stomach. I was about to suffocate. They tied ropes to the shackles on my ankles and yanked them abruptly. My ankles hurt so much. Sweat, tears, and blood soaked my hair and clothing. Later, I fainted because I couldn't bear the pain. Then they poured cold water and boiling water over me to revive me. The boiling water scorched my entire body. I couldn't stand the incredible pain and wished they would just shoot me.

"Each of the seven policemen then smoked three cigarettes at the same time and blew the smoke into a bucket put over my head. I couldn't breathe and passed out. So they poured cold water on me again. When I was barely conscious, they pressed lit cigarettes against my eyeballs. Then they punched me in the head, face, and nose, and knocked out some of my teeth. My face swelled up and turned dark purple. They also stuck thin bamboo sticks into my ears to puncture my eardrums. I couldn't hear for over two weeks after that…

"They tortured me three times in seventeen days in that devil's den. The torture was more brutal each time. Once, the police didn't want others to see how badly I had been tortured, so they covered me with thick clothing. But the blood soaked through it. So they put more clothing on me but the blood soaked through again…

"Later the police took Ms. Guo Shuaishuai and me back to the prison hospital and launched a new round of persecution there. We were tied to a bed. The police then gave me an injection of some unknown drug, and I've had no feeling in my legs ever since. My legs turned ice-cold and numb.

"It was horrible to see the process whereby a person is tortured to death. Ms. Guo and I were stripped naked and tied spread-eagle on a bed. Policemen and male prisoners lewdly stared at our naked bodies every day. One of the male prison doctors pinched and groped Ms. Guo's vagina. Unable to bear it all, Mrs. Guo ate a spoon. She tossed and turned in bed from the pain. The prison doctor cut open her stomach to take out the spoon, deliberately made an unnecessarily long incision from her chest to lower pelvis, stitched her up roughly, and sent her home to die.

"As for me, I was transferred back to the detention center because I refused to renounce Falun Gong. The detention center wouldn't accept me, though, because they heard I was about to die and feared having to take responsibility for my death. Outraged, the police hung me over a door for six hours and beat me. Then I was taken back to the prison hospital for more persecution. I went on a hunger strike in protest. On the fiftieth day of my fast, one of the prison doctors used a knife to cut open my vein and put an intravenous needle into it. My blood spattered on the bed and floor. Having grown accustomed to seeing bloody persecution, the police and prison doctors were not at all disturbed by the excessive bleeding. They pumped ten bottles of unidentified thick fluid into me every day and left me to relieve myself right on the bed. For days I lay in a pool of feces and urine…"

Chang Xuexia is an extremely gentle and quiet young lady. She lowered her head in shame when recounting her painful experience in a labor camp:

"Because I petitioned for Falun Gong I was illegally detained for thirty-nine days in a labor camp in Dalian. They locked me in a small metal cage and brought in a variety of torture devices to try to get me to renounce Falun Gong… Several of the prisoners hung me by the wrists with my feet barely touching the floor. A woman by the name of Wang was giving the prisoners orders, saying, 'Fix her good, all of you!'

"The swarm of prisoners struck and kicked me from all sides, and I passed out. They dropped me onto the floor and stomped on my face and arms to see if I was faking. When I woke up, I couldn't move part of my left arm, as my elbow had been dislocated. The prisoners who refused to torture me were transferred elsewhere and had their sentences extended.

"Later they hung me up again. This time they put a photo of Falun Gong's teacher in my underwear, and wrote things slandering Falun Gong and its founder on my face. They also beat me with a hard wooden plank. The bruises are still visible now, even after a year.

"This didn't convince me to renounce Falun Dafa, though. They stripped me naked, and several of the prisoners began pinching my breasts, plucking my pubic hair, and jabbing my vagina with a brush used for cleaning the sink. Then they put a basin under my lower body to see if I was bleeding. Since no blood came out, they decided to try using a bigger brush and repeatedly jabbed my vagina with it. I couldn't bear the excruciating pain any longer and succumbed to one of their demands—I said I wouldn't do the Falun Gong exercises at the labor camp.

"But what I experienced in the camp was not the worst of it. Another practitioner named Ms. Wang Lijun was tortured in one of the small metal cages. When she was in the cage, some of the prisoners pulled a rope with knots in it back and forth in a sawing motion across her vagina. Her entire lower body swelled up. The guard in charge then ordered the prisoners to jab her inflamed vagina with the sharp end of a broken mop handle. This made her bleed profusely. Her abdomen and vagina were so swollen that, afterward, she couldn't put on her pants, sit, or urinate. She couldn't walk normally, either. I also witnessed the prisoners using the same torture on a young, unmarried girl. The guard in charge even put poisonous insects on some of the female practitioners' bodies."

A thirty-five-year-old man from Dalian told us the following:

"I started practicing Falun Gong in 1998. Because Falun Gong teaches people to live according to the principles of Truthfulness, Compassion, and Forbearance, I've become much better as a person, both mentally and physically. I know how to forgive others easily and also improve myself morally. So after the government began suppressing Falun Gong in July 1999, I couldn't ignore the fact that our fundamental human rights were being violated, and went to Beijing to file a petition for Falun Gong. When I got on the train, I was stopped by a police officer and asked to say negative things about Falun Gong's teacher, Mr. Li Hongzhi. I refused, so was arrested. Afterwards, I knew that whoever traveled to Beijing at that time, whether by train or by bus, would have to say something negative about Mr. Li or Falun Dafa; otherwise they wouldn't be allowed to travel.

"...Three other practitioners and I were taken to the fourth floor of the Dalian Labor Camp, where they tried to force us to defame our teacher and Falun Dafa. Those who complied were taken downstairs to write the 'three statements': one defaming Falun Gong and Mr. Li, one criticizing themselves, and one pledging not to practice Falun Gong again. Those who refused were punished with electric shocks. They stripped us and handcuffed me to another practitioner named Liu, with us facing each other. Using six electric batons, they shocked us on our heads, backs, thighs, genitals, both sides of our chests, and necks. We clenched our teeth and contorted our bodies to try to avoid the electric shocks. Because we were moving like that, the handcuffs kept tightening, eventually cutting through to the bone…

"The electric shock torture continued for about an hour, and then they separated us. They handcuffed Liu's hands behind his back and made him crawl on the grass. Then they put two chairs on his back and asked two criminals to sit on the chairs. After that, another six prisoners used six fully charged electric batons and repeatedly shocked his back, buttocks, neck, calves, soles of his feet, and genitals, all at the same time. They even pulled out his penis to shock it specifically. As for me, I was tied to a chair and shocked with six electric batons simultaneously. My body was convulsing and I felt as though I'd rather be dead. People said my desperate screams could be heard throughout the entire building. I was told that the many Falun Gong practitioners held on the second and third floors wept when they heard me scream.

"After about an hour of this I was made to change places with Liu. Once again I was shocked with six electric batons at the same time for about an hour. I felt like I couldn't take it anymore, but I knew I would rather die than betray my beliefs or deny my conscience by defaming my teacher and Falun Dafa. So I started ramming my head against the floor, hoping to knock myself unconscious. Every time the six electric batons touched me at the same time, it felt as though a thousand arrows were being shot into my heart.

"I felt like I died several times over. After the electric batons ran out of power, they switched to new ones with a higher voltage. At that point I became afraid and succumbed. Later, Liu couldn't endure it anymore and succumbed, too… So we were taken downstairs to write the 'three statements' against Falun Gong. When we returned to the work team, we had to write those same three things every day, over and over, defaming Falun Gong and its founder, and we had to shout them out every day, too. It was killing me from the inside. The pain was far worse than that of the physical torture. But if we refused to do it, we would be taken to the fourth floor to be shocked until we succumbed again…

"Over time I realized I couldn't cooperate with the guards anymore. So I stopped wearing a prison uniform, stopped marching, stopped singing, and started a hunger strike in protest. My whole work team decided to join in the hunger strike and protest with me. Later we were separated, and I was sent to the third brigade where I continued the hunger strike. When a chief prosecutor asked me later why I started the hunger strike, I said that I had no other recourse, as no court would dare accept my case. I told him that the courts and judges all belong to Jiang Zemin, that no one dares to represent us, and that the only thing I could do was to use my own life to protest my treatment and to protest Jiang Zemin's persecution of Falun Gong.

"I have a son, and when one day in the future my son asks me, 'Back when the innocent people were being horribly persecuted, what did you do?' I don't want to have to tell him that I yielded…"

As I listened to the vivid descriptions of those who had escaped death's clutches, I could hardly breathe under their weight. To those whose uniforms bear the symbol of this nation, I say, "How many of these ruthless acts have you committed and covered up?"

Mr. Hu, Mr. Wen, and all fellow Chinese: It is time for every one of us to take a good, hard look at ourselves! In the history of the world, never has such a huge group of people suffered such severe and long-term persecution during peacetime, simply on account of their faith. This disaster has cost thousands of precious, innocent people their lives, and has deprived hundreds of thousands of their freedom. This utterly inhuman persecution has caused over 100 million Falun Gong followers and their families to suffer. How absurd, treacherous, and immoral this is! It is an onslaught against the Chinese people, civilization itself, and the very moral fabric of the world!

What has happened to my law firm and my family has made abundantly clear that those in China today who stand up and speak the truth will pay the price. Time after time, the state has used violent means to tell people that a desire to understand or speak the truth is a very dangerous thing. As the regime has matured, so have its mechanisms for hiding the truth. As a result, even members of the regime themselves aren't able to know the whole truth anymore.

People like Ms. Wang Yuhuan and others who suffered in labor camps witnessed the following time and again. When higher authorities came to inspect, those who might speak the truth, such as Ms. Wang, were taken to a place where inspectors could not find them. As soon as the iron gates closed behind the leaders as they left, the crimes being committed against our innocent fellow countrymen resumed. There is a collusion between the inspector and the inspected, both of whom know the truth, though it be left unspoken.

This makes investigations by citizens themselves imperative. We have the right to know how this persecution began six years ago. And over these six years, exactly how many innocent citizens have been illegally imprisoned? What, exactly, has happened behind the high walls of the prisons and labor camps? It is the moral obligation of us citizens to seek and obtain answers to these questions. In fact, many who know the answers to these questions are already among us, and are working tirelessly to expose the truth.

Our investigation has shown that, in dealing with people of such steadfast faith, those assigned to "transform" them have lost their humanity. A clear example is the recent, horrifying incident in Hebei province in which a policeman raped two female Falun Gong practitioners in front of his colleagues.

The Chinese police have turned into out-and-out criminals. The concepts of justice and a legal system are far removed from their minds, and they operate under the assumption that their duty is to prey on people. Moreover, they have lost the fundamental sense of shame that is inherent to being human.

Our investigation has also shown that the forced labor system is another source of vile crimes, and one that has brought about tragedy many times over the last half-century. This underhanded system, which is run by the State Council, has survived despite its flying in the face of constitutional principles. It demonstrates that the government's claim of ruling the country according to law is a hoax. The forced labor system is the greatest obstacle to China's achieving rule of law. Our investigation demonstrated that the way the labor camp system abuses and deprives people of their freedom is beyond imagination. Ms. Wang Yuhuan, despite being an older woman, and Ms. Sun Shuxiang, were both illegally detained nine times in six years. The procedures are so informal as to be laughable.

It is time for the government to fess up. I would like to stress that if this evil crime does not stop, then the day when Chinese society is stable and harmonious will never come. People have lost their patience with the power-abusers who cast aside their conscience at will. As a result, a storm of peaceful protests has begun to challenge the status quo in this country, which the people have been tolerating for decades. How could this not be taken seriously?

Meanwhile, in communicating with people of such conviction, I saw them demonstrate qualities invaluable to our nation. The fact that they were able to describe their horrible experiences with a pleasant countenance and a calm tone of voice left a deep impression. I found myself moved to tears. I am finally seeing people in this country with an unyielding spirit and a resolve to protect something dear to their souls. These six years of persecution have fashioned a group of people unparalleled in character. The realm of mind they demonstrate through the solidity of their faith, their contempt for the atrocities they endure, and their optimism about our nation's future has earned my deepest respect.

Another unmistakable pattern we observed in our investigation is that every Falun Gong believer who had emerged from police custody—however long the detention, and whatever he or she said or did while there—became even more resolute in faith. The example of Ms. Han from Fuxin city is typical. She had been arrested multiple times and suffered in custody for several years. After she was released, the local police chief paid her a visit and tried to make her promise not to practice Falun Gong anymore. She told him firmly, "Even if you arrest me one hundred times, I will continue to practice. Cultivating ourselves is not wrong, much less is it a crime. After returning home after my illegal detention, I didn't let up in telling my family and the people around me the truth about Falun Gong. As a result over thirty of them are now practicing it."

During my time with the Falun Gong group, I discovered another delightful fact. Although society as a whole has declined in terms of people's character, conscience, morality, humanness, and responsibility, quite the opposite has occurred for these people—their spirits have changed in a new and positive way. It's as if they have come from a bygone era. One can sense the power of faith to change the soul. Indeed, this has given me hope that our nation can be rescued from its current, depraved state.

These individuals have little concern for their name or for material things. They continuously and quietly assist other practitioners whose lives are in danger. Their patience in helping the children or older family members of detained or deceased Falun Gong practitioners is beyond imagination.

Here is an example of their great spirit. Thirty-three-year-old Zhu Xiaoguang told me that when he was first thrown into prison, the only interaction among the prisoners was of a malicious sort. A prisoner could gain the upper hand by being more brutal than others. Later on, some Falun Gong practitioners miraculously raised the prisoners' consciousness and ended up helping one hundred of them learn Falun Gong. "I gained an inner calm by transforming my heart," he said.

Former prison guard Zhang Linyou had an even more astonishing experience. He told me that practicing Falun Gong led him to become the only guard in the gigantic Gongzhuling Detention Center who would not torture prisoners or accept bribes. The first year that he stopped engaging in these things was an agonizing period, as he found it very hard watching his colleagues accept bribes while he himself was so short of money. Later, the sixty prisoners under his charge expressed their gratitude and said that all Chinese police should practice Falun Gong. If that happened, the prisoners said, the Chinese police would be the most civil in the world. Despite this, Zhang was later dismissed from his post and sentenced to forced labor because he practiced Falun Gong.

What has been most absent in this country over the last few decades is a foundation of faith, as it is what helps sustain and reinforce the moral values of a people. This is the source of the chaos China has experienced in recent decades. For the sake of our country's long-term well-being, therefore, freedom of belief must be protected. Only if people's hearts change can the world change into one of hope. The government's violence over the past six years, however, has had the opposite effect. It has impeded our nation in its progress toward a better future.

I am not asking the government to reinstate the good name of the Falun Gong. For in their hearts, and in the hearts of those in the world who have a conscience, they know that there is nothing problematic about their group. In addition, a system that has tormented a nation for over half a century is in no position to reinstate anyone's good name. I offer a stern warning to those who refuse to change, who keep perpetrating violence, who keep committing atrocities against those who speak the truth: Stop harming our country's people! That is your only way out!

Finally, with all due respect, I would like to say the following to my fellow countrymen Hu Jintao and Wen Jiabao. You must summon the courage and moral strength to admit that every part of the political machinery used to torment our people over the past half century is stained with the blood and tears of the innocent. You must summon the courage and moral strength to admit that there is no end in sight to the misery of the Chinese people, who have lived under oppression for thousands of years. You must summon the courage and moral strength to admit that our people have the right to pursue democracy, freedom, the rule of law, and human rights, and that this desire has never been as fervent as it is today. You must summon the courage and moral strength to admit that any attempt to obstruct people's pursuit of these rights in China today will be in vain. Pardon my frankness, but you cannot deny that the bloodshed our people have seen and experienced remain in their memories.

Gentlemen, a word of advice. Only when we take the safety of our afflicted fellow citizens to heart may we be truly safe. Likewise, only when you genuinely care about our nation's future will you have a good future.

May the new year bring Hu Jintao and Wen Jiabao peace and good health!

May the new year bring a world of difference to all fellow Chinese!

God bless the Chinese people!

Your fellow citizen,

Gao Zhisheng
Changchun city, Jilin province

The Gao family

五

The Siege on My Family: A Journal

Some notable figures in China have suggested that it's futile to record daily the details about the agents monitoring me. They say it tarnishes my image. While I would not encourage others to do as I do, I think it would be wrong not to record these encounters. I have always believed that the unlawful actions whereby agents of the Party stalk people, harass them, and place them under house arrest violate basic ethics and human rights. I consider it my responsibility to record such things, to bear witness to actions so base, and to expose the cruel tactics of the Party.

November 23, 2005

Early risers of a different sort

The truth regarding the bizarre persecution of my family

Thirty-five days have passed since the publication of my letter to Hu Jintao and Wen Jiabao wherein I raised my concerns about the wrongful persecution of persons of faith by local governments. And it has now been thirty-three days since the government began its unlawful and despicable practice of subjecting my family to what is practically around-the-clock surveillance.

At six o'clock this morning I stepped outside, about to take my daughter to school. With my appearance, government agents who had spent a cold night outside quickly sprang into action. In less than thirty seconds, six or seven agents raced towards me left, right, and center. They saw that I was getting my bicycle out, and realized what I was planning to do. They then dashed to their cars and motorbikes, which were parked outside the community gate, and waited there. After my daughter and I passed through the gate, the entourage quickly caught up with us. The motorbikes kept a steady distance of about ten feet from us.

My daughter asked me, "Dad, there must be something wrong with their brains! What's the point of following you when you take me to school?"

"There is nothing wrong with their brains," I replied. "They don't have any."

"But how could someone live without a brain?"

"In China, living without a brain spares a person suffering."

My daughter said she was puzzled.

"My dad is a good person. Those people who are following you are like shameless hookers," my daughter quipped.

We both laughed. My daughter went on to tell me that at school there is a song going around that pokes fun of such women, and that now she wanted to learn it so that she could sing it to the agents tomorrow.

I said to her, "I'm jealous of those agents. You've never sung for me!"

She responded with a serious tone. "It's a humiliating song."

We soon arrived at the school's gate, having chatted the whole way. I had to help her to her classroom, since she had recently sprained her ankle. One of the agents followed us inside.

On my way back home I passed by Yuandadu Park, and decided to go into the park for a morning jog. The agents thought that I was trying to run away, and went into a panic. They shoved their motorbikes aside and raced after me afoot. At some point it must have dawned on them I had no intent of "running away," for they settled down. They still followed me closely, though, keeping just a few yards away. What really amused me about it was that, much like what happened the day before, there was one agent among them who at all times would report my movement to the group's superiors. "Ah, yes, he's now at such-and-such junction..." "Ah, turning eastward..." "Turning southward..." "Yes, he's putting his left hand into his pocket!" "Okay, his hand is now out of the pocket..." "Now he's at the traffic light..."

This reminds me of something ludicrous that happened yesterday afternoon.

On that day my usual trip to pick up my daughter from school threw the agents and their superiors into complete panic. My tight schedule means that I'm always racing against the clock, and picking my daughter up from school is no exception.

I thus raced down the stairs yesterday and was about to hop on my bicycle when the agents spotted me. They went berserk, running about and shouting. "Quickly! Hurry up! Hurry up!" "Quickly start your cars! Quickly rev up motorbikes!" "Hurry, some of you quickly follow him on foot! Quick!"

Two minutes later the unmarked Sonata that had been tailing me the past few days came to a screeching halt in front of my bike. The other cars that were following me arrived, too. Next came the motorbikes. There were two agents to a bike. On one of the bikes was a guy who appeared to be the leader, as he was constantly reporting my every move to some unseen boss. The whole fiasco left quite an impression on me. They acted as if the regime's survival depends on their being able to track me down at every second. It's as if the fate of the nation hung in the balance of how quickly these agents reacted. A few of them came close to barging into my office when I went there to work after dinner.

As of the 20th I discovered that there is a human side to the agents' superiors. Every night my "guards" are accompanied by pretty ladies. This probably explains why the agents remain so loyal.

As I write, these agents are still carrying out the unlawful and sordid measures enacted against my family.

December 16, 2005

Like a sudden gust, police appear

Returning home after completing a seventeen-day investigation

At quarter to seven this morning I went downstairs, planning to exercise. This immediately irked the group of plainclothes police who were stationed outside, keeping surveillance on me. Nearly twenty cars were getting into position outside, bearing license plates from different provinces; these were the vehicles used to tail my family members and keep watch over us. When they saw me coming downstairs and setting out to jog, the plainclothes officers reacted as if up against a formidable foe. They swooped in swiftly, abandoning their planned division of labor. It was only after they discovered that I was just getting morning exercise, and wouldn't cause any "harm," that they simmered down and reduced the agents following me to four.

While I was returning from my morning exercise one of the agents began to vent. He told me to behave myself and warned that I should mind the look in their eyes. If I didn't follow this advice and something bad happened to me, "Don't say you haven't been warned," he said.

I asked him, "Are these orders from your boss?"

He said they weren't.

I followed up, asking him, "Didn't you defy your boss's orders?"

"That's enough nonsense out of you!" he snarled. "We're all grouchy after spending the whole night out in the bitter cold."

I sternly told him, "You really have a pitiful life." Tellingly enough, he looked puzzled.

When I arrived home, my wife had apparently noticed the arrival of our "guests"; she indicated that she had sent some hot water downstairs for the agents to drink. Our housekeeper didn't understand this and remarked that it's really not necessary to show concern for "those rotten eggs." I told her that we were showing our compassion for these young folks, and that we do so regardless of who they are or what they are doing. I added, though, that we too were disgusted with them!

The situation has now reverted back to how things were when I left Beijing. Plainclothes police encircle our doorway and stare intently at whoever comes or goes. Each time I go out no less than four agents follow me closely. It's apparent they learned a lesson last time (on November 29) when they were shaken. They tail me closely, with the greatest attention. When I went to pick up my daughter this afternoon, again four vehicles followed closely. When I went into the school, the agents went so far as to run after me. Presumably this is what they mean when they speak of their "great professionalism"!

December 21, 2005

Leave the Party, I tell my police "friends"

Today was a frigid day in Beijing. And yet those dear agents who have, because of me, lost their personal freedom still dutifully stood watch outside my office building. The biting wind clearly took little pity on these lives.

The roar of winter's wind has struck fear in plenty of persons this year, but has proved impotent with others. Those agents, for one, will not change their plans on account of cold weather. But that's of course because those who could change their plans are off somewhere inside, content with their own warmth.

The agents who stand watch near the homes and offices of "targets" are not, however, the only ones with no choice over enduring the cold. There is another group that finds itself in a similar circumstance, but for a very different reason. That is, the tens of thousands of compatriots who have come to Beijing to petition authorities! The persons comprising this group have long been denied a normal life or a taste of warmth. But this dreadful winter they have, in coming to visit me in Beijing, brought me a certain kind of warmth.

Some two dozen head petitioners from various areas paid me a surprise visit at my office today, saying they wished to visit me during this time when authorities harass my family so severely. We had a nice talk, and they expressed a hope that the agents outside could hear my impromptu speech. On that note, I thought I would share my remarks with the agents outside, and thus raised my voice as I said the following to the visiting petitioners.

"First, I would like to thank everyone for bringing me and my family warmth and love on this terribly cold day. But I am pained by my inability to help you at present, for you have long been neglected. I am determined to repay what you have given me. I will summon all the strength I have to help you get the warmth and care you deserve.

"I share in your concerns and anxiety. But I'm opposed to the dangerous rhetoric some people have used, which suggests removing the word 'legal' from the term 'legal weapon,' the idea being that a 'weapon' alone can be used to complete the transformation of Chinese society. Please know that I, like you, am eager to see Chinese society change quickly. Yet the change we seek will not only be unprecedented in the kind of social system it brings about, but also in the means used to achieve it—nonviolent resistance. China's history has witnessed all too many violent revolts that brought a momentary jubilation to the oppressed but which never, in the end, saw tyranny replaced by a government by the people and for the people. Never! A change is not complete if it merely meets the needs of the oppressed. Only a change that impacts the course of our nation will ensure that never again is there a class of people that might be called "the oppressed." As for how to bring about nonviolent change, I would say that the Falun Gong have succeeded at finding a means to change that will not lead to the shedding of one drop of blood. And that approach is, to persuade people to quit the wicked Party—a party that has done every form of evil imaginable in this world. My suggestion is to quit the Party and be closer to God! This way we will have both a beautiful kind of change and a wonderful, lasting system afterward!

"It is our misfortune to live in the China of this historical period. No one on this earth has ever had to experience or witness the suffering that has befallen us!

"Yet it is also our fortune to live in the China of this historical period. For we will experience and witness how the greatest people on earth banished this suffering once and for all!

"How quickly change will come to China rests in the hands of the people, and that includes those of you who sit here."

Our meeting thus concluded with a mix of tears and applause.

December 24, 2005

Covert and overt spying

Today they are tailing me with what is clearly greater care than in previous days. When I went to exercise in the park this morning, there were several agents around me at all times, and they stayed close by following me home. After breakfast my wife took our daughter to her music lesson, and sure enough, several agents followed them. During my daughter's entire one-hour lesson the agents stood around outside, strange as it was, before proceeding to follow her home. At noon, my daughter was due to attend an English class at school. As she headed off for class, I saw two secret agents—each both large and tall—promptly head out, following my slender little girl. I was furious that a young child would be subjected to such frightening treatment twenty-four hours a day. I notice in myself a sense of helplessness. Seeing the cruel tactics our government has used on my very own daughter, and the psychological impact all this has had on her, has been downright hard to take.

Lunch with uninvited guests

After our daughter left, my wife suggested that we go out for lunch. This time the agents tailing me showed up in full battle array, what with six cars pulling up out of nowhere. Each had at least two agents in it, one of whom held a walkie-talkie. I pretended not to notice it, and let them put on their absurd show. Once I stepped outside it was easy to realize that someone in hiding was adeptly directing the agents.

Before long we arrived at Kentucky Fried Chicken. As we went about our meal, a large man with glasses and an expressionless face approached us, only to stop just a few feet away from my wife, where he stayed standing. Judging by the blank look on his face and the countenance of the other agents just behind him, I was sure they had done this many times before. So we decided to just go about eating our lunch. As we did, the men continued to stand there, silent, waiting for us to finish. On the way home my wife and I were once again "escorted"—as I've come to think of it—by several cars.

A little while later we went to the office to work. This time, the crew tailing us actually led the way! My wife joked that they could make out my destination just from what I was wearing at the time. That afternoon, as we met with around sixty petitioner representatives from Shanghai, these so-called "secret" agents went on "doing their duty," waiting by the door.

January 1, 2006

On New Year's Day, as unprincipled as ever

Today, the first day of 2006, the plainclothes police and their superiors have shown themselves to be as unprincipled as ever.

This morning I didn't go out. At 12:45 P.M. I drove to a house church to partake in Sunday worship. Joining me in my car were overseas journalists, who are following our story. Among them was a photographer, who was going about his normal procedures and had no intention of photographing the vehicles of the government agents. But when the agents noticed that my companion was taking photographs, what ensued left us doubled-over laughing. Those government vehicles and their drivers just seemed so ridiculous to us today. They appeared like a pack of mice who had just crawled out of their holes for the first time. I say this because they seemed totally incapable of handling what was an unfamiliar situation. For example, as we drove along we were all in high spirits, and a couple of times we slowed down as if about to stop abruptly. The vehicles that were tailing us would quickly prepare to turn around and disappear, hoping to not get caught following us—as if it wasn't terribly obvious what they had been doing. Just about their whole squad moved about in sync. They really were just like timid mice treading on new turf. The whole ride they provided us with amusement aplenty.

The agents' shady ways resumed during my trip home in the afternoon. On the way, a friend and I got out and entered a small barber's shop. The agents quickly proceeded to park their vehicles all around the shop. The agents knew that the reporter who was taking photos earlier had headed off, so they were more confident now, and went back to their unscrupulous ways. They opened their car doors and fired away one snapshot after another of the barber's place. The barber was astonished. He couldn't believe it. He said if he hadn't seen it with his own eyes he really couldn't have imagined that the government could stoop to something like this. Only a lunatic would act like that, he said. I laughed and told him that spending just a day with me would be eye-opening. We all had a good laugh.

January 2, 2006

A new record: twelve vehicles!

Seldom in the past did distinguished guests come to visit my home, but by the grace of God things have been different the past two years. I have played host to quite a few persons of prominence of late. Guo Feixiong, a human rights defender, is one of them.

On October 20, 2005, the government started employing scoundrel-like means, deciding to monitor and tail my family around the clock. When I am in Beijing I make a practice of publicizing each day what the plainclothes police have been up to. This is a practice I've seldom verged from.

Yesterday—the second day of 2006—Guo Feixiong came to my home after having just been released from one-hundred-plus days of unlawful jailing by the dark forces of Guangdong province. We spent many an hour discussing how to carry on our fight for rights, should Guangzhou University decide to forcefully put a stop to our activities. I thus didn't have time to write up the activities of the agents for the day. I realized it when calls started pouring in from around the world this morning, inquiring about yesterday's missing report. I would like to apologize here to my overseas friends for having to await my report. I should also ask the forgiveness of the plainclothes police, to whom I usually give a copy of my report each day. The following is my report for yesterday.

Yesterday was the second day of the New Year. I once wrote that the mindsets of those who oversee and control the agents around me are not normal. They aren't relaxed on holidays, for example, as people normally are. Just the opposite, they are extra tense and nervous. I have proof to support my observation.

I was out and about most all day yesterday, and a total of twelve cars followed me around. That's in addition to the vehicles stationed near my home twenty-four hours a day. A few minutes after I headed out in the morning, I decided to stop my car, get out, and approach the mass of cars following me. Much to their embarrassment, I started to write down their license plate numbers. The agents seated behind the wheel of each car tried to hide their faces, much like whoremongers when rounded up in a police raid. I was surprised by what I found: There were twelve cars in all, carrying thirty six agents—thirty-three male and three female! Their license plate numbers were: Tianjin AX6865, Beijing EJ8520, Beijing H39710, Tianjin AU3651, Beijing A11161, Beijing C12696, Beijing E92673, Beijing EP0030, and Beijing FE6234. There were additionally an Audi and two Mustangs that had no plates. It took me nearly ten minutes to do all the counting. Just doling out their salaries would take half a day, I'd guess.

I went to a dinner for the Independent Pen Association this afternoon, and again a string of cars followed. When we arrived at the event's venue, a restaurant, dozens of members of the association and invited guests were already gathered—all of whom were themselves accompanied by special agents. They weren't afraid of the agents, and decided to take photos of them. The agents scurried off like rats. Waves of laughter rolled through the crowd; people relished the unexpected theatrics. We spent five hours in the dining room, eating, drinking, and talking before finally going downstairs to leave. When we went outside, there the agents were—still dutifully waiting and watching from the parking lot.

Back home, my wife told me that she had to see a photographer for an errand in the morning, and no less than four plainclothes police were on her heels. Now even she is used to being followed!

January 5, 2006

The battle expands

Since November of 2005 the Shengzhi Law Office has been crowded with visitors every day. These persons mainly fall into three categories: persons from throughout the country who represent petitioners; intellectuals from across China, but mainly Beijing; and our friends in the media from around the world.

Those plainclothes police who are controlled by behind-the-scenes bosses have not, for their part, sat idle amidst this. Starting from around October 20 of last year, nearly two dozen of them have come to act as my personal "bodyguards," as I call it. When I am at home they mill around near my home. When I am heading to my office they follow me closely. When I am at my office they hover close by the entrance. All day, every day, they are there, stone-faced and with cameras in hand, ready to photograph anyone who comes to see me. This is apparently meant to scare visitors off. How ironic, then, that the number of visitors has increased! The plainclothes police wonder to themselves, baffled, "How come nobody is afraid of us?"

For the duration of this morning I met with at my office, surrounded as usual by a large number of plainclothes police, representatives of petitioners from Beijing, scholars, and human rights activists—a dozen or so in all. We discussed matters of human rights in the coming year. We agreed upon an initiative to be carried out nationwide and that would conform to existing guidelines on the promotion of human rights. Namely, we will encourage all petitioners and rights activists throughout the country to partake in local elections where people's representatives are chosen. We shall pool our resources in Beijing and set an example for the rest of the country. A heated discussion ensued, related to election procedures, potential candidates, strategies for organizing support groups, and other details. We were completely oblivious to the police around us, who were trying to assert their presence.

My associate Guo Feixiong told me that he had been followed this afternoon by two or three unmarked cars. I should thank him, then, for diverting part of the force that tails me.

January 7, 2006

"He's a Falun Gong!"

Twelve cars with a load of nearly thirty plainclothes police have followed me around, with some of the their crew being terribly arrogant. I took a picture of the worst one of them. I hope the people of China will remember his face.

A friend who came to my home today felt really upset upon seeing the arrogant and craven behavior of the plainclothes police outside. He decided to quietly use his camcorder to tape the crowd of men tailing me and my family. And indeed, we managed to capture three faces on our tape. Afterwards we thought over what effect publicizing their images would have on their lives, and decided against releasing two of them, so as to protect them. We thought they were probably too young to know the indecency of their conduct. We thus made public just one of the figures—the one who repeatedly tried to intimidate us up close. He had even threatened us with physical harm.

Goodness, these clowns are amusing. We know that our "adversaries" are crazy and not like normal people, so we decided to make four copies of the footage, and proceeded to hide them with different persons.

At around four o'clock in the afternoon, I was on my way home, accompanied by two friends. As we walked through a crowded and noisy market, we discovered that half a dozen plainclothes police were following us. The market was just a few hundred yards wide, and with street closures, it had only one exit. It seemed as if the police were moving in on us. This was just too much, we thought. We took out our video cameras and started shooting their harassment. One of them looked at me in surprise. He then turned to the others, pointed his finger at me, and shouted, "He's a Falun Gong. He's a Falun Gong!" Dozens of curious onlookers had begun to gather around by now. People can see from our footage that the craziest agent was fuming by that point, and had begun to physically shove us. I managed to stop him.

Enraged, he yelled at me, "Tape me again, and I'll have you arrested and locked up for fifteen days. If you don't believe me, just wait and see! Bastards like you are the dirtiest f__ing lives on Earth!" He did this as I was explaining to the crowd the infringements my family, and even daughter, had been subjected to. Oblivious to the crowd, the agent kept pacing back and forth, shouting and cursing.

It was no accident the plainclothes police acted so madly this afternoon. They were no strangers to the neighborhood, after all. For seventy-three days now they had been hovering around my home, just two hundred yards away, in their chosen spot. Their tactics at the market—and in particular shouting out "He's a Falun Gong"—were meant to show local residents they had a reason for hanging around all those days. And after having labeled us Falun Gong members it would seem natural for them to arrest us. They further tried to find grounds by provoking us. They first aimed their own video cameras at us, and then hoped to catch us throwing fists at them. But their plan failed. Two policemen did indeed get in my face, and even pushed and shoved, but I managed to stop them without getting physical. And we remained calm as we explained ourselves. Whatever new scheme they come up with, it's not going to work on us. Tellingly, the agent who was so enraged vanished after yelling about us being "Falun Gong" and threatening arrest.

This was the third time in the seventy-three days of tawdry, gangsteresque, state-run monitoring that my personal safety was put at risk. (The previous two times, plainclothes police had attempted to ram my car.) Incidentally, the dictatorship sent word to us, via a friend, that they would "handle" Guo Feixiong when he left town.

To those persons behind the scenes, running the machinery of China's dictatorship, I want to say the following: You should know that we who are rights advocates have formed into one cohesive body. You might "handle" Guo Feixiong today and me, Gao Zhisheng, tomorrow, but are you capable of "handling" all of us? If you dare to play with fire, we will never cease to haunt you as long as you are on this earth. Maybe you can imagine what will happen, but you could never guess how soon it will be. You have warned us not to cross the line. Well, we warn you in return not to cross our line.

I hope that those of you who read this will still have the presence of mind to share this with your superiors.

January 11, 2006

Guo Feixiong's exit

Today, January 11, Guo Feixiong left town with many police tailing him. We thus had another chance to witness the unusual strength of the police's numbers set against the abnormal weakness of the regime as it tries to govern.

This morning, a Beijing freelance writer came to visit me in hopes that he could take some pictures of the police cars and plainclothes officers that monitor my family. I agreed to it.

I told this friend, "Of the 6 billion people on this earth, nowhere are more spies and plainclothes police found than in China. Today you, my friend, have the luck of meeting the individual who is monitored by the largest number of spies and plainclothes police on this planet." My new friend was excited, if not downright astonished, to see so many unmarked cars outside. And this time, there were police cars with sirens and flashing lights, bearing "security" plates, springing up outside my home. This was a first. How funny it was, then, that when my friend took pictures the police cars tried to avoid him like mice scurrying away from a cat.

After my friend left, I approached one of the unmarked police cars and rapped on the window. The four policemen sitting in the car were so scared, no one dared to respond.

So I kept rapping on the window. One of the four finally opened the window cautiously. I told them to relax. I explained that my car was broken, and asked them if I could borrow their car to take Guo Feixiong to the train station since they would be following us there anyway.

They said that they couldn't make such a decision. One of them wasn't as nervous as the rest, and asked, "Could we talk with you?"

I responded, "Sure, why not? I never refuse to talk to anyone."

"Aren't you leaving with Guo Feixiong?" he asked me.

"No."

"But we asked the ticket office, and they indicated that you purchased four tickets to Hubei. Who will be leaving with Guo, then?"

I replied, "I bought only one ticket. Guo is leaving by himself."

"We thought you'd bought four tickets and were going to Hubei to investigate Falun Gong related matters. We have been so busy of late. We were hoping we would get to rest a couple days after you left with Guo."

"Well, I too would like to see you take a break someday!" I said.

Another policeman then asked out of the blue, "You're always having meals with so many different people. Where does the money come from? Who pays for the meals?"

"Sorry," I said. "It's your job to find that out. I'm not going to do your job for you." Thus ended our curious conversation.

Guo later headed out of town, escorted, sure enough, by a full group of plainclothes police. Guo smiled at the affair, full of confidence and determination.

January 13, 2006

The most shameless of villains

After seventy-eight days of being stalked by the Party, my family and I have come to the conclusion that the plainclothes police of China are the biggest and most shameless villains in the world. I could imagine that not that many people would object to this statement, strong as it may be.

Today in broad daylight, this repulsive group again showed just how despicable it really is.

At noontime today, January 13, my wife and I were about to go to lunch with a group of attorneys who are friends. The minute we stepped out of my office plainclothes police surrounded us. As we came downstairs and exited the elevator, police were there waiting for us in the lobby. They followed us out of the building. Then when we stepped outside, a plainclothes policeman was sitting in an unmarked car, filming us with a video camera. This kind of thuggery has gone on for over seventy days now!

I happened to have my video camera with me, and so I began filming the man in the car. He sprang from his car and jumped on me, screaming, "You bastard! Don't you know it's a serious violation of human rights to videotape someone? I'll beat your ass if you don't stop!"

It was a sight to see this grown, six-foot man turn so emotional and lose control. More than once he berated me and screamed. My wife, our attorney friends, and I stayed calm throughout his tirade. I told him, "Please, calm down! I'm a Christian and I won't swear at you. Besides, we're both over forty and we shouldn't wildly swear at a person." He wouldn't stop yelling or swearing, however.

Twice he aggressively shoved me as well as Jiang Tianyong, an attorney who was standing beside me. Jiang tried to calm the man down, and beseeched him not to keep shoving. But again it was to no avail, for the man then pointed his finger at Jiang and began yelling at him. As more and more onlookers gathered around, this undercover policeman increasingly lost control of himself. After we had tried reasoning with him for some twenty minutes or so, he then pointed at me, and barked, "You've violated my human rights, you bastard. I'm going to call the police and have you arrested." To nobody's surprise, after but one phone call the police had rushed to the scene. Next thing we knew Jiang and I were being whisked away in a police car.

At the police station we were escorted to an office, where lo and behold, the very same plainclothes policeman was present. Again he lost his wits and leaped forward, swinging at us. Another officer who was present intervened and stopped him. The officer then began to record whatever I said. I told the policeman: "This person and a dozen other plainclothes police have been flagrantly stalking my family with the most sordid of means for seventy-eight days now. Do you have the courage to tell them to leave?"

"Can't do that," replied the policeman.

I followed up, asking, "Since you can't stop his unlawful conduct, then what qualifications do you have that would allow you to bring me here?"

The police held us for an hour. While at the station, the same plainclothes policeman said, his tone menacing, "Just wait and see how I fix you once you leave."

Jiang then told the other police present there, "You heard that. You'd better escort us home with a police car."

I told Jiang, "Let's not do that. I'm curious to see what he tries to do after we step outside." We quickly followed behind him after we got out, but by then he was gone.

January 14, 2006

Have they any way out?

The recent spate of irrational behavior by the plainclothes police suggests that their bosses still haven't reached their goals, despite laying siege to my family for nearly eighty days now. There are indicators that their patience is running out. But more significant is that I can tell, as the target of their shenanigans, that they are now losing confidence.

This morning I was busy doing an interview with the German weekly *Spiegel*, so I asked a friend to take my wife and daughter shopping with my car. Since it was my car that they took, the plainclothes police were as tense as when I set out, and so seven of their unmarked cars closely tailed the car. My friend later told me that the seven cars followed them wherever they went. When my friend parked the car and went shopping with my wife and daughter for a couple hours, the seven cars could be seen—filled with dozens of bored police—lined up, waiting, near our empty car.

I was amused this morning when I left my building. An entourage of about twenty persons had formed before I was even out of my neighborhood. As we passed a nearby market, stall owners who witness a scene of this sort every day winked at me. A dozen or so young folks at an auto repair shop came out to watch. Most of them know me by now. One of them asked, "You're followed by plainclothes police every day. Aren't you afraid?" I showed them the video camera I had in hand, and replied, "Here's my magic weapon. I scare them off when I aim it in their direction."

With that I turned and raised my arm, pointing the camera toward the pack of undercover police. Sure enough, they ran off in every direction. Crowds of people began to watch. The police were conflicted, not wanting to leave me, but feeling a need to scurry whenever I pointed my camera in their direction. Dozens of onlookers were now on hand, laughing hard and cheering from the sidelines. When I turned the camera on them a fourth time, what did I see but that the two dozen police had covered their faces with women's shawls. Only a thin slit for the eyes remained open. This was clearly an expedient they came up with after the previous day's encounter. The crowd of onlookers had by now swelled to around two hundred people. The hilarious scene had them in stitches, laughing, whistling, cheering and jeering. This was the first time in nearly three months spent in my neighborhood that the plainclothes police had brought residents something positive—laughter. One onlooker yelled out, "My dear plainclothes police, won't you come back again tomorrow!" The crowd had a really good time of it.

Soon after I had lunch, some journalist friends from Kyodo News came by. When I arrived downstairs and stepped out to greet them, a completely different scene met my eyes: All of the plainclothes police were gone. A sort of sadness came over me. They had been with me for seventy-nine days, and now, just like that, they had left. As I was coming to terms with this, a large number of young ladies—similar in number—came into view, swaggering about, trying to be seductive. After months of dealing with these police around the clock I have gained an inexplicable sense of discernment. I am able to identify plainclothes police who follow me with just one glance, wherever it may be, and however many their number. Even if he is a new assignee he won't go undetected. Seeing what was at work, I aimed my video camera at the ladies. The theatrical response it evoked outdid even that of the male police earlier in the day. The women quickly tried to cover their faces with their hands, and turned, trying to face a nearby wall. It was as if their body language said: anything but our faces! The arrival of the undercover female police has added a certain new flavor to life under monitoring these days, but otherwise, nothing has changed.

Our government has sunk that low. It would seem it can survive only with the most crude and criminal of means. Cowardly actions such as theirs of late are completely unheard of in the civilized world. I could sense that over the past seventy-nine days they adjusted their tactics constantly, but with each new fold, their behavior grew only more craven and funny. The only constant all along has been their unlawful practice of tailing me.

I would like to say the following to those who plot and scheme all of this behind the scenes. However skilled you get at following my family and me, you are still every bit as wicked, and you are playing with fire. You are going down a dead end street. Only when you cease with your hostility toward people, toward moral values, toward humanity, toward civilization itself, and toward the very dignity of man, only then might you be able to reconcile with the Chinese people. Failing that, yours will be a most unfortunate end. If you don't believe it, let's wait and see.

January 16, 2006

Love that flows like the Yangtze

January 13, 2006, was the seventy-eighth day the mafia-like, regime-backed police had wrongfully monitored my family. On that day several plainclothes police boasted that they could have me arrested in a matter of minutes if they wished. And indeed, shortly after police took me away. The ordeal lasted about an hour.

I will always remember the 13th as an unusual day, but not on account of having lost my freedom for an hour. The real reason is this: After I lost my freedom for an hour, I received inspiring support from a variety of Chinese persons both inside China and around the world. Word of police having detained me sent ripples like a stone hitting a placid pool. Within minutes of my having been detained, online media were reporting the news.

Dr. Teng Biao and other members of the legal community gathered as quickly as possible outside my home. During the one-hour period hundreds of organizations around the world responded rapidly. I was stunned by the show of support that greeted me upon my release from the police station. By midnight I had answered over a hundred phone calls from Chinese persons around the world. I had to turn off two of my phones for a period of an hour and a half at one point. I was too exhausted to answer any calls.

After my release from police custody, Reuters, Agence France Press, Voice of America, Deutsche Presse Agentur, *The New York Times*, *The Washington Post*, and the BBC all proceeded to interview me by phone. Countless Chinese also called to offer support. All told about a third of the calls I received were from overseas Chinese, with another sixty percent being from mainlanders.

During my hour in detention, around six hundred Christians in Henan and Hubei provinces made a pact, communicated through mobile phone messaging. Their pledge was: "We are prepared to protect Gao Zhisheng with our lives." Meanwhile, in Beijing thousands of Christians decided to fast and pray for me the following day. Later they would show the record of their prayers and fast to worldwide media. Their efforts were to persist until I was set free. There were also a great many workers, farmers, intellectuals, servicemen, and businessmen who phoned me in the ensuing days.

One businessman phoned me from Langfang, of Hebei province, and said, "Mr. Gao, if you had not been arrested I wouldn't be talking with you and would be off working. But with you arrested, our relationship is different, for your case affects us all. Your arrest crossed a line in our minds. We will never ignore your plight. My employees read your articles every day. It was I who initially suggested they read them. Though I'm the head of the business and I suggested they read them, I have never forced my employees to do what I want, nor directed them about in some way. Everyone is entitled to his or her own opinion. Those who wished to quit the Party have done so. We are simply running our business. The main thing is that you, Mr. Gao, are safe."

I also received phone calls from people in Anhui, Yunnan, Shanxi, Sichuan and other provinces. Many people told me, "Mr. Gao, we aren't just all talk and no action here. To support our conviction, we have sent letters to the Ministry of State Security, the Ministry of Public Security, and the Ministry of Justice. We told them bluntly that if Mr. Gao were arrested we would protect him with our lives. We won't allow them to act unjustly."

The outcome of the regime's actions this time was different in many ways from before. For example, lots of professors and college students began contacting me. Some professors provided advice on how I could protect myself. Several professors from Tsinghua University, People's University of China, Peking University, and Henan University discussed how to ensure my security in the time ahead. One group of Tsinghua professors phoned my wife, in fact, to offer suggestions on safety. Many people from the greater Beijing metropolitan area visited my law office, offering support.

The supporters decided to arrange for volunteers to protect me during the time ahead in which I would be mourning my mother, who recently passed away. Furthermore, a volunteer would be there to help me with typing, and a professional cameraman would be arranged to help as well. This morning, some professors from Peking University, People's University of China, and China University of Geosciences visited my office. Several of these older, adult men held my hand and had tears in their eyes. Professor Wan of Peking University had been in a labor camp for twenty-one years; he spent the prime of his life—ages twenty-eight to forty-nine—doing forced labor for no legal reason. These older visitors spoke of the hardship they had experienced on account of the government. A sense of gloom filled my office. The psychological torment inflicted upon them by the government was etched into their faces. And yet, despite their own suffering, here they were, old age and all, moved by a deep concern for my safety.

Over the past few years I have done all in my power with each legal case I've handled. And in return, the love and support given to me during this critical time has seemed as large as the mighty Yangtze River. My heart has been deeply touched, though I know they never had it in mind to win my gratitude. I feel guilty for not having done enough for them. Even if I were to give all of myself to these people, it wouldn't be enough.

January 17, 2006

"Send in reinforcements!"

Yesterday evening I had dinner with my friend Professor Jiao Guobiao at my home. We talked over our meal, and when we had finished, I went downstairs with him to see him off. We said goodnight outside the complex and I started back home. As I turned, I saw two agents around the corner of one building. I could hear one of the two yelling into his mobile phone, "Quickly send in reinforcements. He and Jiao Guobiao have left together." The spot where Jiao and I parted company was just a six-minute walk from my home. Yet by the time I had strolled back home, a massive contingent of unmarked cars and plainclothes policemen had already gathered outside my apartment. It was quite a presence. It looked like a scene out of some action movie, where you have countless police cars swarming around suspected terrorists.

In my judgment, and maybe I'm not right, Jiao is not a fellow who is very impressed by the Party. On no occasion where I've spoken with him has he said anything about the Party being "great, glorious, and correct" or about how it "forever triumphs." (I suppose he could have said such things while not in my company.) I guess the Party isn't about to share any love with the likes of Jiao.

During these eighty-plus days in which government agents have besieged my family, mafia-style, I have managed to receive and see off my guests in a fairly normal fashion. That is, with the exception of Jiao's visit. This one clearly caused the masterminds behind the scenes to panic. And the reason why is no secret.

Between November 29 and December 12, 2005, Jiao and myself—two folks who don't hold the Party dear—"sneaked" off to the northeastern city of Changchun, and there investigated the savage persecution of the Falun Gong by Party apparatchiks. Afterwards, in a twenty-thousand-word open letter I exposed the horrors that the Party's underlings have committed there, detailing how they ruthlessly killed my fellow men and women of faith with means so shameful and cowardly as to be unknown to history. The letter has sent unending reverberations throughout the nation. A sinister force of habit dictates that the Chinese Communist Party will regard whatever heinous crimes its followers commit as just daily affairs, and even brand those who expose their crimes enemies to hastily eliminate. People like myself and Jiao cause their blood to boil, especially when we link up. They haven't yet finished avenging our last trip to the Northeast, and if now we two uncooperative fellows were to again "sneak" off and air the government's dirty laundry, the shining image of the forever "great and correct" communist rulers would be further tarnished.

The pathetic Chinese Communist Party once had abundant energy—enough to commit atrocities as well as cover them up. Now it has just enough lingering strength to commit vicious crimes, but not the resources to convincingly mask its evil. It is approaching its death. The fifteen-day trip I made with Jiao to the Northeast bespeaks of its pathetic state.

People have a hard time grasping the bloodlust of the Party. Common sense would say that if you're afraid of having the horrors you committed exposed, you learn a lesson from it, and never again do inhuman or evil things. Yet reality proves that common sense doesn't apply when it comes to the nature of China's communist regime. Just as a human being lives off of food, China's communist regime is dependent on bloody horrors for survival.

It's well known that since the publication of my three open letters, the regime has continued to savagely suppress innocent persons of faith. This yet again reveals just how wicked and fundamentally opposed this regime is to civility, to morality, and to humanity. It amounts to a taunting of the Chinese people and others around the world who know the truth about its cruel murder of innocent believers these past six years. But nobody should have false hopes. No more could they dissuade the regime from doing evil than could they talk people out of, say, eating.

Recently the provincial government of Shandong unlawfully sent the attorney Liu Ruping off to a labor camp for speaking up for Falun Gong, and made like gangsters in roughing up human rights attorney Yang Zaixin, who had offered to defend Liu. These incidents serve to remind us that this land under communist rule remains today as dark as ever.

The communist regime's inherent hostility toward humanity and rule of law will never change. Those who still have illusions about the regime are longing for what would amount to a day when wolves morph into humans or maybe even philanthropists, who charitably adopt deserted lambs. That is a day that will never arrive.

January 18, 2006

A contrived "car accident"

Last night a Chinese friend from Canada came to visit me. After we parted ways at a tea house, I set off driving for home. It was around 10:20 P.M.—an hour when many fewer cars travel the streets of Beijing. The car ahead of me had its license plate covered over by a piece of newspaper. As soon as I saw this I knew inside that the car belonged to the group that tails me. But there was something odd this night: The car following behind me was a military vehicle. The middle numbers on the front and back license plates were also covered up by a piece of newspaper, I would learn. It was apparent, I could tell, that someone wanted me to know I was being followed by a military vehicle. This was the first time I had been tailed by such a vehicle. Another strange thing was, prior to yesterday I had always been tailed by a big contingent of cars, while last night these two cars were the only ones.

There were few cars on the street at this hour, and we were moving along quite fast. Suddenly the car ahead of me braked—right there in the middle of the street! I braked almost instantly. My car stopped less than an inch from the car ahead of me. Braking suddenly at that speed is extremely dangerous, since any cars behind you will find it almost impossible to stop in time. I got out of my car and took a look. Since the license plate at the back of the car was covered, I ran around to the front to catch a glimpse of the front plate. To my surprise, the car suddenly started up and drove right at me! I jumped out of the way with a speed that surprised even me. I lost my balance as I was dodging it, though, and my right hand landed on the car's hood. I used its momentum to propel myself out of the street, and landed in a curbside garden. Had I been even just slightly slower, the military vehicle would have run me over. As the car which attempted to hit me fled the scene, the newspaper covering its back plate fell off. The exposed number read Beijing EB8233.

Only after both cars had fled did fear have time to sink in. This was a fear that ignored my will. It was a visceral fear, one that made my heart race. I stayed there in the garden, squatting down, for about five minutes. I then went back to my car. I sat in my car for six or seven minutes, alone.

Suddenly, the two vehicles appeared again, like phantoms, this time both in front of my car. I sprang from my car and pounced on the car that had tried to run me down. I moved with a speed that took the driver by surprise, and yanked the newspaper covering off the front license plate. Before they could react, I pounced on the military vehicle. I was about to tear the paper cover off its license plate, when the driver snapped out of it and suddenly put the vehicle in reverse. It then sped off. Both cars retreated about four hundred yards. Then, a moment later, they turned around again and began driving toward me, slowly. At this point I got back in my car and drove home.

After I arrived home I talked with my wife. She said she remembered something about a car with the license plate Beijing EB8233 from before. We looked into it and determined that it was the very same car that had followed me on December 30, 2005.

January 18, 2006

Reminiscent of the Cultural Revolution

Often there are people saying: with the development of the economy and citizens becoming conscious of their rights, the Chinese Communist Party is sure to, given time, turn good again! But that notion is just utterly at odds with the reality of the Party! When it recently used a slew of absurd measures against my family and me, it revealed that much hasn't changed. For example, when it persecutes someone, it is so sinister as to kick that person when he's down. Consider its practice of investigating several generations of a person's family.

Last night, a man who used to be my colleague twenty years ago at the Wiredrawing Factory of Kashgar, in Xinjiang province, took great pains to call me. While we talked he revealed that two judges from the Kashgar municipal court approached him. They were attempting to investigate my conduct back when I worked at the factory—twenty years ago. This former coworker told the investigators, "About Mr. Gao Zhisheng, our factory can offer two sentences of appraisal: first, he is a good person; and second, he is extraordinary for someone self-educated. We've heard that he has become a prominent attorney in Beijing."

Things seem to happen in pairs. This morning, another coworker from twenty years ago called me as well. This one informed me that a certain workplace in Kashgar brought him in, wanting to ask about what I was like twenty years ago. My former coworker relayed, "The investigator acted secretive. Seeing this, we figured you must have stirred up something big. We're calling since we are all concerned about you." If the Party occupies itself investigating me off thousands of miles away, trying to find "problems" on my part twenty years ago, how can we look upon those well-dressed powerbrokers of today's Party with any respect? Even supposing I had committed some awful crime or done something twenty years ago, the law stipulates that after twenty years the statute of limitations expires and I cannot be re-investigated. However, the Party went thousands of miles to dig up some "crime" from twenty years ago. What value would determining that have? And what's more, the mere fact of the legal system's having had a hand in investigating me is itself a violation of the Constitution and the Organic Law of the Courts. What repulsive news this was, then!

A short while ago, some departments of the central government also went so far as to launch a large investigation to find "issues" in my life some ten-plus years ago—in Urumqi city of Xinjiang. The facts they arrived at with their "investigation" left them embarrassed. For example, they discovered that in 1999, thirteen government entities—including the Political-Legal Committee, the People's Congress, the police, procuratorate, and Court of Xinjiang province—enthusiastically awarded me the title "Xinjiang Province Top Ten Defender of the People." (I can't recall the exact details, but do remember that there were thirteen large seals on the honorary certificate, which I chucked in the garbage after getting home.) Also, they learned that at the end of 1998 the Judicial Bureau of Urumqi City had awarded me with a medal of "Third Level Merit." At the award ceremony officials present included those from Xinjiang's Political-Legal Committee and an office of the Judicial Bureau. The Party-run newspaper of Xinjiang, the *Xinjiang Daily*, along with another paper, *Long Journey to Justice*, both reported on my accomplishment. Reportedly the Beijing investigators who discovered all of this had long faces at their findings; this wasn't quite what they had planned on digging up.

The feedback I've gleaned from different locations has made it clear to me that, for one, this persecution against me is systemic, and secondly, that the mastermind is no ordinary figure. The following prove illustrative. One cadre from Zhejiang province was promptly summoned by the Public Security Bureau simply on account of having twice called my home. He was reprimanded with a stern warning. A teacher from Henan province was summoned by the local police department and interrogated for six hours, simply on grounds of having made a phone call to me to offer support. A cadre from Guangxi was likewise called in for interrogation just for having shown himself supportive of me! And then there is the friend from Xinjiang who, after calling me several times out of concern, had his home stormed by police a few nights back and his family threatened. Every day I receive phone calls to this effect.

All of which should be sufficient to remind us: the Party is mobilizing its resources throughout the nation in order to persecute me. And secondly, it suggests that the mastermind behind it all is not apt to be just another run-of-the-mill committee member of some central government department. He is at least someone with the rank of a member of the Standing Committee of the Politburo.

The purpose of their terribly overdone persecution is undoubtedly to suppress the growth of activities by citizens to protect their rights! They don't fear so much me the individual as the demand for legal rights from the Chinese people that the movement is apt to awaken. Notably, the Party has no interest whatsoever in initiating a rational dialogue with the Chinese people so as to resolve their different opinions. Rather, it has already made the sinister determination that it must continue to murder and suppress "with all means and at all costs."

That kind of decision does nothing but harm to our country, to our citizens, and to the Party itself. The lust for power and profit has turned those persons into something demonic! They stubbornly stick to their foolish assault on human decency. Theirs is a dead-end path.

February 20, 2006

Beijing's insane policeman

These days I get the sense certain leaders of the Beijing Public Security Bureau ("PSB") wouldn't hesitate to cut my family's throats, if only they had the right tools and means. These Party officials undermine the very concept of being human.

Several days ago, more than a dozen uniformed officials from the Beijing PSB brought into the police station the female manager of a barbershop where my nephew works. They interrogated her for nearly twenty hours, obscenely trying to conjure up some sort of "scandal" involving her and me. The next day, the Beijing PSB kidnapped Wen Haibo, my assistant attorney; Wen has never broken any law. After being unlawfully jailed for a day, Wen was then put under house arrest by officials from the Beijing PSB and their thugs. They told him that if he didn't stop working for Gao Zhisheng he would live out the rest of his life under house arrest.

The day before Wen was arrested, policemen from the Beijing PSB and their thugs broke into my office. This was a first. They kidnapped our volunteer staff member Ouyang Xiaorong, who at that point had been working for us only twenty-four hours. Ouyang is a father with a family, and it has now been five days since he was seized. His whereabouts are still unknown. My wife and I are worried for his safety. We fear another Sun Zhigang[1] tragedy. What unjust and inhumane acts will China's police not commit?

On February 15 another recent volunteer at my office, Mr. Ma Wendu, was arbitrarily thrown in jail. Ma was held for forty-eight hours. Since his release he has been under house arrest. The same day as his seizure, Beijing police disconnected my mobile phone, my home and office phones, my fax line, and Internet. Most days I still can't go online. Daily nearly a hundred policemen, secret police, and similar thugs prowl about outside my home and office, all so as to keep people such as Ma and Ouyang from helping me do clerical work.

These throngs of police have become a mindless tool for venting the regime's hatred. They will obey any order as long as it takes aim at me; none of them weigh the legal or moral implications of their actions. One day a regular Beijing citizen came by to ask me a few legal questions about renting. Lo and behold, afterwards secret police followed him home, and the very next day broke into his home, hoping to find that his family had failed to register its residence.

Government officials have sunk to the point that they now have no sense of honor; so above the law are they, they don't care how others see them. Just today a Beijing man named Zhang Wanhe wanted to visit me, but was blocked by a pack of poker-faced plainclothes police. The police and their thugs keep creating tension and terror around my home. All that's left for them to do is to figure out how to slit my family's throats. And I wouldn't even doubt certain people are working on this!

---

1 Sun Zhigang was a young college graduate and fashion designer who was beaten to death by Guangzhou city police while in custody. He had been detained for failing to produce an identity card required of out-of-town workers; he had forgotten to carry it that day.

February 22, 2006

"Whoever gives him subsistence money..."

The siege laid upon my office and home shows no signs of letup. Throngs of rogue-like secret police still teem around me and continue to use indecent means to stop whoever tries to meet with me. Since yesterday the telephone at both my home and office, as well as my fax line and Internet, have all been cut off. Even the Web function on my mobile phone (which allows me to go online) has been disabled, and for a good seventy-five percent of the day my mobile's status is supposedly "in conversation."

Today, Beijing PSB officers went so far as to photograph and perform body searches of whoever tried to visit me. These persons were unfortunately arrested by the gangster secret police in front of my office. These brave citizens were threatened, questioned, and physically accosted by the Bureau. The officers would say things such as, "Didn't you provide for Gao Zhisheng's living expenses?" "Nobody is allowed to provide Gao with any subsistence money. Whoever gives him subsistence money will be sentenced. You shouldn't offer him any money, even if he's starving to death."

The would-be visitors who were interrogated told me later by phone, "Mr. Gao, it's so despicable. How could government agents casually say such awful things? They would yell at us, 'Gao Zhisheng is rotten. His family deserves to starve.' We were terribly upset!"

February 23, 2006

A chat with the Beijing Judicial Bureau

On February 23, 2006, after many days of silence, the Beijing Judicial Bureau finally ordered me to come in and discuss the matters at hand. Again it was Chai Lei who asked this—a man who finds great pleasure in others' misfortune. I share here the content of our conversation.

Chai Lei: Mr. Gao, we haven't met for a few months. You look better than last time.

Gao Zhisheng: Thank you. Since breaking from the Party my mind has been at peace and my life more smooth. In my heart I truly have a sense of freedom like never before. This inner spiritual freedom, along with the freedom to travel, has allowed me to move forward with my life. I have written quite a bit recently.

Chai: Have you thought about examining your political behavior over the past few months?

Gao: Why yes, I have 'examined' my behavior. But the sort of examining I do isn't the kind you have in mind. The 'examining' I do every day is written down and published.

Chai: We've read what you wrote. Let's go to the conference room and bring others into the conversation.

(A total of four people, myself included, then went into the conference room.)

Chai: Mr. Gao, your license to practice law hasn't been officially revoked yet. You are still a lawyer, strictly speaking. It's just that you have been made to stop practicing law.[2] Since you are still a lawyer, your conduct falls under the jurisdiction of the Judicial Bureau. We have the authority to bring you in for a discussion.

Gao: I haven't questioned your authority to ask me to talk with you.

Chai: Look Mr. Gao, you're a smart guy. Let's put it is this way: At present there are certain lawyers who are acting out of line with the constitution and the law.

(I then interrupted Chai.)

Gao: Chief Chai, you need to be more specific. Who's this fellow that has violated the constitution and the law? Do you mean me?

Chai: What I said was 'certain lawyers.' I didn't name you specifically.

Gao: Chief Chai, you seem to have made a mistake. Whoever it is you have a problem with, that's who you need to go and speak with directly. It sounds like I'm not the guy you find at fault. If you have a problem with other lawyers, you really need to go and talk with them directly. Your questions don't quite make sense to me.

2 By this point Gao's law firm had been closed by authorities.

Chai: You're a smart guy. The person I am talking to right now is you. You should be able to figure it out.

Gao: Thanks for the compliments. Since you are a government official, any conversation between us is a matter of public record. Why do you keep playing cat and mouse with your questions? You are trying to suggest that I've violated the constitution and the law? Let me ask you this: As we discuss today, do you represent the Chinese Communist Party or the Beijing Judicial Bureau?

Chai: I'm of course representing the Beijing Judicial Bureau.

Gao: Chief Chai, it looks like you've again made a major mistake. As you are a representative of the Beijing Judicial Bureau, you have authority only to determine whether my conduct as a lawyer is correct and within the guidelines stipulated by the Bureau. If I have indeed violated the constitution or the law, and even if I violated Chinese criminal law, then only those government departments that enforce those laws should be dealing with me. You've far overstepped your responsibility as a government official. If a government official has overstepped his responsibility by that much, then it is his behavior that violates the constitution and the law.

Chai: Look, I want to be clear with you. Do you really understand what you are doing? Do you really understand the consequences of your activities of late and your answers here today?

Gao: Chief Chai, again you've made a dumb mistake. You are threatening me. The Party has already tried to threaten and intimidate my family and me. There are nearly a hundred special agents of the regime who continue to harass us on a daily basis. They have been acting absurdly, devoid of shame, for almost one hundred days now around the clock. All of their efforts have been futile. They haven't even scared my daughter. Do you really think your feather-light words here today are going to intimidate me? I think you've seriously miscalculated.

Chai: You haven't been cooperating with us on your punishment, either.

Gao: There you go again, talking nonsense. We've all been waiting to see the Bureau's supposed 'reorganization' and 'discipline.' To date, we haven't seen either take place.

Chai: Haven't you already appealed our decision? You needn't go on as you are. You'll get a good response to your appeal.

Gao: Mr. Lei, let's bear in mind these are strange times we live in. Our conversation today is merely the product of present circumstances. I'm not awaiting some response from the Judicial Bureau. Your only real concern here is your own job security. But my life and the actions I take are different: They are based on higher principles.

Chai: All right, do you have anything else to say?

Gao: Every day there is something to say. But today you ordered me to have this conversation. I didn't ask to speak with you, so I don't have anything further to say.

Chai: All right then, let's end the conversation here.

With that, the conversation ended and we parted.

Feb 27, 2006

Ending the violence and hatred

How strange that someone who doesn't see others as his enemy would be regarded by another as the supreme enemy. But such is the mindset of those who have besieged and harassed me for a full one hundred days now. Irrational hatred fills their hearts.

Chinese people seem to be fond of certain numbers. Five, ten, fifty, and one hundred are examples. Often people choose dates with these figures for major events, be they national celebrations or just regular weddings.

China's communist regime has now laid siege to my family for one hundred days, making a show of unlawful and base means. Even though the government is doing it with total disregard for my well-being, I felt that I should—after friends who work in the media reminded me that today marks the hundredth day of the siege—put something in writing.

The average person won't detect any difference between my family and any other typical Chinese household. The one difference is, of course, that for the past hundred days and nights, communist police have done everything in their power and wracked their brains to make us "special." The "dutiful" work of the police has brought my family unimaginable hardship.

For these one hundred days police have acted as if confronting an opposing army, rather than one lone individual. Yet an objective look at my conduct reveals that I've done nothing beyond speaking a few words of truth. And I have revealed only the very tip of the iceberg, no less. I have but scratched the surface of the cruel suppression of Chinese people's lives, spirits, and freedoms.

These men of the regime are decked out in Western suits and talk all day long about "building a harmonious society." But witness their furious, irrational, and shameless response to my open letters. It's just not comprehensible.

In its attempt to show me its sweeping and omnipresent power, the regime has spared no effort these past hundred days. It has used as many as forty cars to tail and mob me on so-called "sensitive dates." The personnel used on me has grown from an initial dozen per day to more than a hundred. The routine and lawless badgering has quickly evolved into what is attempted today: to deprive my family of even its most basic needs.

This is demonstrated by two things. First, they prevent me even from renting out part of my own home, which would provide some income to support my family. And secondly, since February 15 police from the Chaoyang Branch of the Beijing PSB have tried everything possible to deprive my family of a means of survival. These one hundred days my family hasn't received so much as a penny from our visitors, yet authorities wrongly claim that they support us financially. Police then carry on arresting whoever visits me or whoever I try to see. This kind of harassment is not just shameless, but unlawful.

They have even arrested my attorney, Dr. Xu Zhiyong. They kidnapped him and took him to the police station, where he was held for three hours. Whoever they arrest they ask, "Have you ever provided financial support to Gao Zhisheng?" They further threaten whoever they abduct, and force them to write a "statement of guarantee" promising they will never support my family financially. What a shame that the government, which is supposed to be honorable, openly acts in such a lawless and sordid manner.

The police have done countless vile things to us these one hundred days, even using violence on me. I really hope they can calm down and reflect on what they get out of all this. The Party knows full well the police's conduct these one hundred days has been outrageous. That's why they have kept quiet and not launched a propaganda campaign, as you would normally expect.

These past hundred days I've not only had to face police harassment, but also criticism from a number of citizens who consider themselves "sensible" and just can't keep quiet. What's most surprising to me is that these "sensible" people have shown themselves to be so patient when faced with the dictatorship's cruel abuse of rights advocates who hunger strike, yet they got all worked up over our use of nonviolent resistance. Here I don't wish to criticize their silence over abuses by the dictatorship. But I would observe that they seemed to find in our plight a rare opportunity to show the world just what "sensible" people they are.

But these "sensible" people betray a warped kind of thinking. One such person is named Liu Lu, and hails from Qingdao city. So riled up did Liu get that he claimed he could, if necessary, compile a long list of people who disagree with the relay hunger strikes. Was he talking nonsense, then? You would really have to be something to come up with a long list of Chinese intellectuals who do dare to take a stand against tyranny. But finding intellectuals who don't dare to oppose tyranny is all too easy. You could come up with not just one long list, but many. Voices such as Liu's are not the exception.

Another example would be that of Ms. Liu Di, from Beijing. Liu claimed that conditions in China aren't ripe for a nonviolent rights movement, given that China lacks the kind of civil society and open media that Mahatma Gandhi and Martin Luther King, Jr. had. That logic was shared by Mrs. Ding Zilin, who completely discounted the value of international support to the hunger strike. Liu meanwhile overlooked the impact of the Internet and international media, and failed to appreciate the large volume of responses from throughout the country within just forty-eight hours of our hunger strike's announcement. Could that have happened without the use of mass media?

Independent media did help Gandhi and King more speedily achieve their goals. But does this mean that in the absence of an independent media the Chinese people can never achieve their goal of defending their rights in the face of tyranny?

I know full well that the road ahead of me will not lead to power and privilege, and nor is it free of peril; and I know full well it does not curry favor with the powerful or bring with it limitless perks. My road is paved with snares and thorns. It is colored with the blood and tears of those who have walked before me. Indeed, in this land where tens of millions suffer today, someone like me will surely not have it easy.

The past one hundred days are but the beginning of my ordeal. But through these long days I have stayed true to my faith in Jesus, and have thus not been alone. As it has been said: "If God be for us, who can be against us? Who shall separate us from the love of Christ? Shall tribulation, or distress, or persecution, or famine, or nakedness, or peril, or the sword? Nay, in all these things, we are more than conquerors through him that loved us. The night is far spent; the day is at hand: let us therefore cast off the works of darkness, and let us put on the armor of light."

It is for the sake of this land called China that we make our way through the ordeal with light, and endure. Ours is a path that leads to a glory and justice arbitrated finally by God. To the one who plans to harm my family in the days ahead, I offer a word from the Bible: "It is mine to avenge; I will repay."

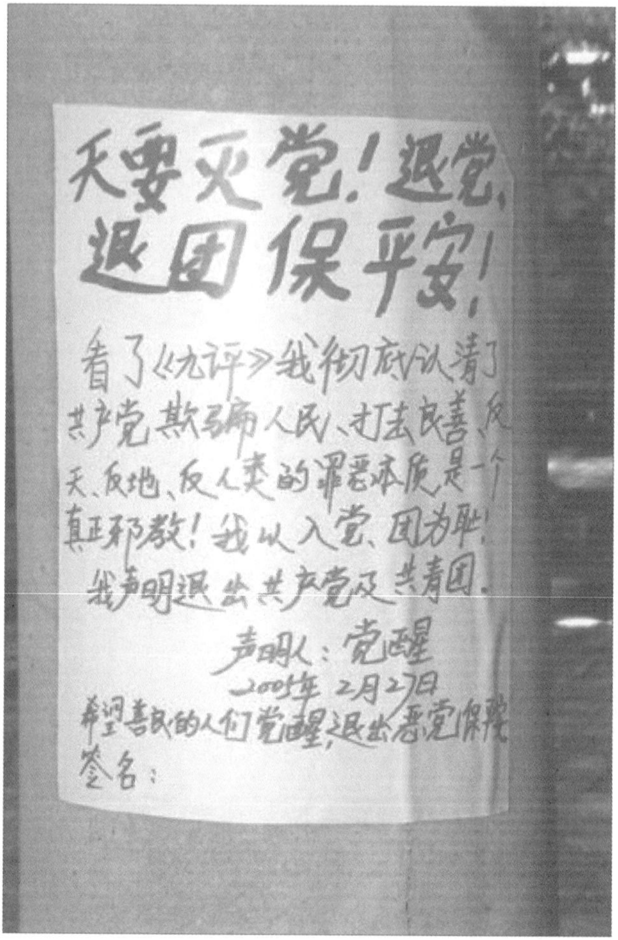

Statement of withdrawal from the Chinese Communist Party, posted in public. Tens of millions have withdrawn in recent years.

六

Breaking from the Party

My Wife Quits the Party

In her own words

My husband and I became members of the Chinese Communist Party while serving in the People's Liberation Army back when we were young, energetic, and naïve. The pressure to join the Party grew if one did not do so within three years of entering the service. Everyone thought that those who didn't join were bad people, and any soldier who did not join could not walk proudly.

We never imagined that our Party membership would end up restricting us from doing things; much less did we know that this affiliation would become such a dark stain, deep in our souls. We later became more cognizant of what was going on, and so over the past five years I have refused to participate in Party activities and have long since stopped paying Party dues. According to Party regulations, my membership should have been automatically revoked years ago. But the Party never removed my name from the roster, as continuing to list the names even of people who have left the Party allows it to continue claiming it has some 70 million members. Now my spirit, moral bearings, and innermost soul no longer allow me to continue with this charade and urge me to formally declare: I, Geng He, hereby withdraw from the Chinese Communist Party.

For roughly eight years, my husband and I have witnessed how this organization has continued to bring calamity to countless ordinary Chinese people. In recent years, millions of our compatriots have sought to petition higher authorities because the Party's savagery has hurt them to the point that they have absolutely no way of sustaining basic living conditions. But their petitions have been met only with flagrant persecution, and we simply cannot tolerate this anymore. The barbaric oppression of those who have any kind of faith, especially the ruthlessness with which our Falun Gong compatriots have been treated, has persisted despite continued criticism from the civilized world. Other Chinese people of conscience now also face escalating persecution.

The Party has made sure to set a most awful example for people, and made itself ubiquitous, thus ensuring that its evilness is planted deeply in people's minds. Deep down, everyone knows that this is the current situation, but the Party still tries to force people into believing it is "advanced." The recent Preserving the Progressiveness campaign[1] made it clear to China and the world that the Party still plans to continue down the same old path for a long time to come.

For about eight years, my husband and I have persistently done the best within our abilities to assist the people we have come across who suffered cruel persecution. The resulting oppression and humiliation we have experienced is beyond words. Especially since last year—because we have been providing support, financially and in spirit, to those who have petitioned higher authorities and to those innocent Falun Gong compatriots who have suffered persecution—as the Beijing Judicial Bureau's Vice-Chairman and the Beijing Bar Association's Chairman

1 In this campaign, Party members must swear their loyalty to the Party and attend frequent "study sessions."

have unleashed inexplicable fury on us. They have openly persecuted and threatened us with a range of extreme measures.

The Temporary Residence Permit system[2] has long been considered the Chinese equivalent of racial segregation. However, following the outcry over the 2003 incident in which a Guangzhou worker was beaten to death after being caught without his permit, the offensive system has basically been brought to an end. Yet, just a few days ago, Public Security staff came to our home to examine our family's Temporary Residence Permits. We said to them, "We live in our own house that we bought and have property rights to. How could we possibly be temporary residents of our own home?" But the police scorned us and said they would return to investigate in a few days. Since then, over ten plainclothes policemen have closely followed my husband and monitored our house every day, giving me a deep sense that all is lost.

The way the Party has always dealt with those who—having already endured ruthless persecution—remain unwilling to acquiesce, is to use even more barbaric and more obscene methods of persecution. All we have done is to lawfully stand up against the way we have been persecuted. Something that makes the Party's behind-the-scenes plot even more unfathomable to the free world is that the Ministry of Justice has launched a secret investigation into my husband's entire life, hoping to incriminate him by contacting his former employers and examining his family background, his previous conduct, whether or not he has previously committed any misdeeds, his political stance, and why he has gradually become a "bad element" who no longer obeys the Party.

Like most decent Chinese people, our hearts are deeply pained by the long-term abuse of our fellow countrymen and by the vicious force's destruction of our nation's long-held values. I now openly proclaim that

---

2 To legally reside and work in a Chinese city, one must possess either a permanent or temporary residence permit. Failing that, one may be removed at any time and be denied equal rights to public services.

I sever my affiliation with this Communist Party organization, which has completely lost any sense of reason and is far from being humane or civil. I hereby completely remove the deep, dark mark that the Party has embedded in my soul!

I have come to realize that continuing to maintain my Party membership would run counter to the values that we Chinese hold dear, and to our sense of justice. In fact, it would amount to continuing to cooperate with the cruel oppressor.

Geng He
November 15, 2005

The Proudest Day of My Life

For many days now I've been working virtually around the clock to investigate the recent, savage persecution—by the clique that controls our government—of those who assert their freedom of belief. Today I am bringing this inquiry to a temporary close.

Because my wife and child remain alone at home, and because they are being watched twenty-four hours a day by the most notorious and most immoral policemen—policemen who dare to do anything—every second of my spare time has been filled with worry. May God keep them safe!

Working closely with Falun Gong believers over these past ten-plus days has shaken me to the core. Professor Jiao Guobiao and I have been spending twenty-four hours a day living and eating with groups of Falun Gong believers, people who have emerged from an utterly inhuman persecution having gained eternal life. Professor Jiao said "I feel like I'm dealing with ghosts, because each of these people has died multiple times." To which I replied, "We're dealing with a group of saints. Their indomitable spirit, noble character, and breadth of mind that allows them to forgive those who use violence against them tells us that there is hope for China. These are also reasons why we must persevere."

Over these past fifteen days I have learned of indescribable violence brought upon these kind people. Consider how police and Party cadres treated Ms. Wang Yuhuan, a peaceful old woman. For six years they endlessly assaulted her body and spirit with methods so cruel they make one's blood boil. Time after time, twenty police officers took turns torturing her for over twenty-four hours until they became exhausted and desperately mad. The whole gamut of torture instruments was used to torture Ms. Wang, an older woman, three times in seventeen days. She was once tied to the "tiger bench" for three days and two nights straight.

By the time the two weeks were over and I had finished hearing about these experiences, I began to lose all hope in the Party. This Party has employed the most savage, most immoral, and most illegal means to torture our mothers, torture our wives, torture our children, and torture our brothers and sisters. The Party has raised torture's political standing to becoming an integral part of a Party member's job. The Party is continuously trying to torture out of people their conscience, kindness, and human dignity.

Today, I, Gao Zhisheng, a Party "member" who has not paid membership dues for a long time now, and who has been absent from Party activities for many years, formally withdraw from this inhumane, unjust, and evil Party.

This is the proudest day of my life.

Gao Zhisheng, Dalian city
December 13, 2005

On the Verge of Collapse

(Excerpted from an interview with U.S.-based Sound of Hope Radio, July 1, 2006)

Currently there are only five or six communist states in the world. This number itself shows that communist autocracy is on its way out.

The way the Party is carrying out the July 1 celebrations marking its founding undoubtedly reflects the anxiety and vulnerability that the Party feels at its core. In mainland China, whenever the Party says anything, very few people actually believe it—and this holds true even for the Party's own members. Many people, however, have compromised and shown their weakness by joining in the Party's celebrations.

CCTV broadcast an absurd news piece that said eighty-five red trains would be put into service across the country on July 1 in order to celebrate the Party's birth. I saw the newscast as I was walking by a market. As soon as people saw that piece of news on the television, "ha ha!"—they burst out laughing. Chinese people can clearly see the hopeless situation the Party is in. It just keeps blabbering on and on about things that no one cares to listen to.

I remember what President Hu Jintao said at the Party's Central Politburo meeting in late February: "Our Party is facing a deadly crisis, and this crisis has not eased in recent years; it has intensified."

Party leaders have always sought to build up, rather than downplay their so-called merits and strengths. But Hu's words, at least on that occasion, revealed some truth—the Party is staring death in the eyes.

It still currently holds an entire country hostage, no doubt about that. It needs support from people's hearts to rule the country and ensure its own survival, but right now, the only support it can muster is from those who have neither human heart nor soul.

In one of my recent essays I wrote that if someone told me a year and a half ago that the Party would be abandoned by the Chinese people in a few years I wouldn't have believed it. But if today, right now, someone told me the Party was going to fall tomorrow, I wouldn't be surprised in the least.

The Reasons for Chinese Society's Most Acute Conflicts and the Party's Rapid Demise

Chinese society's most intense source of conflict is none other than the Party's presence. The Party is at the root of all of Chinese society's conflicts and is the guiding force behind these conflicts. All of the present conflicts can be settled only through the process and end result of getting rid of the Party.

The Party's brutality and violence are the most powerful catalysts for its rapid demise. I explained in one of my essays that the Chinese expect very little of their rulers. How little? There's a saying that goes, "Better to be a dog in peace than a man in war." So the attitude is that as long as the authorities can guarantee that I'll be a dog and leave me in peace, I'm perfectly content being a dog.

But today, the Party doesn't even let people dream of being dogs in peace. For example, take Chen Guangcheng's case, in which, under the world's gaze, police openly resorted to gangster-style violence. I brought this up with some people who had been sympathetic to the Party, blindly believed in the Party, or pretended to support it. They, too, were dumbfounded for once. They said, "We keep telling people that the Party is good, and that even if there are some bad members, those are individual cases." This time, though, they recognized that the police acted like the mafia, and that the open use of violence shocked quite a number of people. They couldn't come up with anything to say. How could they possibly argue that using gangster-like means is reasonable?

The Main Problem the Party Brought China

The main problem that the Party has created for China during its long rule is the deterioration of morality and loss of humanity. When it comes to the process that is necessary in order for our national spirit and morality to be revitalized, the question of how exactly to end the tyrannical rule is merely a technical one. When this tyranny does come to an end, however, it's not as if China will make an instant leap and the level of morality will promptly soar to a level befitting a civilized nation. It's not going to be that way. That's because the damage the Party has inflicted upon Chinese people in terms of morality, humanity, and civility is going to plague our people for several generations. So this is the most serious, menacing, and distressing problem.

Conditions for Rights Advocacy in China

Those who are acting to protect Chinese people's human rights are doing so in response to the Party's crimes. In addition, how the Chinese people have treated Falun Gong practitioners underscores the need to protect the practitioners' rights. The victimization of the Falun Gong is something Chinese people know about deep down within, yet refuse to acknowledge. Be it inside or outside China, the Falun Gong have, without relying on others, been dauntlessly and persistently telling people about the persecution they have faced. This has become the most important resource for getting the international community to really start paying attention to the situation in China, and in particular to the present condition of human rights and the advancement of democracy and rule of law.

Furthermore, over seventeen years have passed since the 1989 Tiananmen Massacre, and it can be said that the terror instilled in people because of the large-scale massacre has begun to fade. So some people are now standing up and taking a close look at the fate of the nation.

Another important factor is that the Party's despotic behavior has reached the point of utter lawlessness. Starting last October, I've been conducting an in-depth investigation into the Party's persecution of the Falun Gong. To put it bluntly, everyone knows that the Party is scum, but people don't know quite the extent to which it has departed from humanity, from human dignity, and from basic ethics.

As I have completely stopped my normal legal practice over the past six months, I've been able to devote myself, body and soul, to closely monitoring social issues and observing the Party's conduct. So these conclusions are based on my surveying multiple perspectives, up-close inspection, and firsthand experiences.

As far as Chen Guangcheng's case is concerned, many people have become aware of the same things. His lawyers have been facing daily assaults since arriving in Shandong and have received constant beatings during the entire process of dealing with the local government. When they recently visited Chen's wife, a pack of unidentified thugs savagely beat them. It took them ten phone calls to get the police over to her home. When the police finally arrived, however, they didn't intervene—they just watched as the thugs continued to beat the lawyers. The lawyers' car was even overturned. I helped out financially later on.

There is one more important detail. After the police arrived, bystanders noticed that the officers had removed their police badges and identification numbers. I think they themselves knew that their behavior resembled that of organized criminals and would tarnish the police's reputation.

This whole scenario demonstrates how the regime has only one recourse left—violence. Not the type of violence usually employed by the state, but the kind that gangsters, members of the mafia, and ruffians use. In fact, the Party itself is aware of the situation, and that's why it has resigned itself to this present, hopeless state. The Party uses the means of gangsters to control the people, but, whenever it has a choice, it doesn't do so openly; rather, it does so while wearing suits. This is the situation that has emerged as the Party nears its end.

A Nationwide Movement to Oppose Violence

Chen Guangcheng is just one individual. But even the Party can't deny that his detention and formal arrest triggered a nationwide movement to resist violence, and that this movement is spreading fast. Why did the Chen incident trigger such a reaction, you may wonder?

I should emphasize that although Chen is blind, he can plainly see that the entire Chinese nation is sinking deeply into an abyss of wickedness. He sees it very clearly. When he realized how wicked the Party was, he offered to help others in his midst who, like him, found themselves being persecuted and rendered helpless. After being persecuted, Chen dared to stand up and speak the truth, while people around him dared not. This is the difference between him and others.

When you think about it, it doesn't really make sense for the Party to fear a single individual, and a blind man at that. But what the Party fears most, and thus relentlessly suppresses by exhausting all means, is the indomitable spirit of resistance that insists on speaking the truth.

Most Chinese people have noticed this, too. They've noticed that the Party's purpose is not merely to do away with this one individual, Chen Guangcheng, but to eliminate this precious spirit that is so rare in China today. So it is under these circumstances that this incident sparked the nationwide effort to oppose violence.

Can the Party Reform Itself?

Today, the Party may want to reform itself, but nobody is able to do that because former leader Jiang Zemin managed to do away with any chance of reform. In today's China, anyone with the least bit of cognitive ability can see that Chinese leaders Hu Jintao and Wen Jiabao have two choices before them: One is to abandon the Party, and the other is to persist with one-party dictatorship to the death. There is simply no room to maneuver in terms of reforming the Party.

These are the only two options that lie before Hu and Wen, as the conditions necessary for transforming the Party simply do not exist. If, then, they lack the moral courage to forsake the Party, they will meet their own end along with this run-down state apparatus.

It is now obvious that Hu and Wen are both ashamed of having to put up with this Party; their consciences are constantly plagued by China's rampant corruption and violence. Events like the Chen Guangcheng incident or the northern Shaanxi oilfield incident are continuously testing to see where people's basic morality and ethics are. But Hu and Wen feel they have to protect those responsible for the violence. "You have to support us," these people demand of the leaders. "Otherwise you're putting the Party and the country in jeopardy."

Increasing Party Membership?

Although it's not surprising that the Party claims its membership has increased to a total of 90 or 100 million, this is actually an empty figure. Many, many people have already completely abandoned the Party in their hearts.

The Party is organizing a number of large-scale and elaborate celebrations right now. This simply reminds all of us that its inner nature hasn't changed one bit. By covering the earth and blanketing the sky with violence and deceit, the Party hopes to hold Chinese people's thinking hostage to the idea that the Party will forever be "great, glorious, and correct."

The Party's efforts to increase its membership recently showed up in my family. My daughter told me that her school had asked all the students to join the Communist Youth League. I told her that although I dislike the Communist Party, and both her parents have withdrawn from the Party, the choice is ultimately hers to make. She said the teacher had told the class that those who joined the Party would have bonus points added to their university entrance exam scores, while those who didn't would have points subtracted. It was an outright threat. Think about it, what's the point of having people join the Party ranks like this?

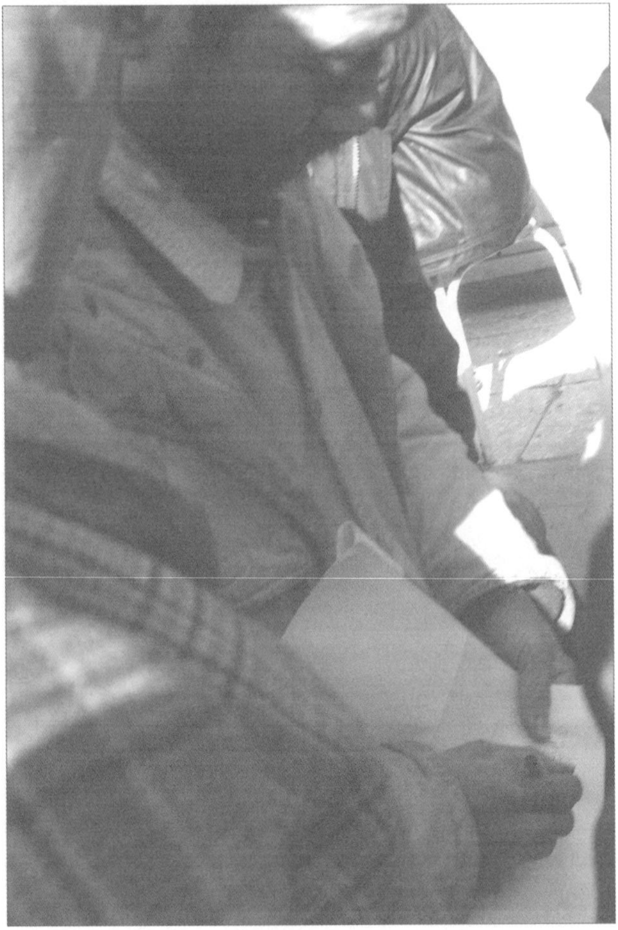

Beijing residents sign up for the hunger strike, March 2006

七

The Hunger Strike Movement

Initiating the Hunger Strike

Gao Zhisheng and Company Propose to Establish a Hunger Strike Group to Support Human Rights

February 4, 2006

In recent years China's communist regime has been perpetrating terribly base crimes against citizens who seek to peacefully and lawfully defend basic human rights. Measures include savagely—and illegally—beating, abducting, jailing, and even murdering. All of this signifies the coming end of the brutal dictatorship that despises humanity and defies all that is civil and moral.

No component in this sinister system is more complicit than the corrupt judicial apparatus. The Public Security Bureau, the People's Procuratorate, and the courts have, absurdly enough, somehow become violent tools that in fact stop citizens from exercising their right to petition the government. Avenues for citizens to defend their rights have deteriorated dramatically over the past half-year.

In the case of the Taishi village, for example, the malevolent powers of the Guangdong provincial government proved terribly aggressive when acting against peaceful citizens. The central government's ensuing silence then encouraged the powers in other areas to act in similarly wanton ways. Witness the violent assaults against Professor Ai Xiaoming and attorneys Tang Jingling and Guo Yan; the detention of more than ten villagers and attorney Guo Feixiong; violence assaults on prominent human rights activists in Beijing, such as Zhao Xin, Qi Zhiyong, Xu Zhiyong, Hu Jia, and Li Fangping; the threats made to this attorney himself; and the violent attacks on Chen Guangcheng in Shandong province. And, in recent days, still more incidents have followed: Secret police again encircled Guo Feixiong's family, tailing his wife and child, as well as photographing and videotaping the two; the violent assault on Tang Jingling and Guo Feixiong; and the assault that citizen Chen Hua was victim to in Shangdong province, simply for having visited Chen Guangcheng—a blind man who has himself been monitored by Shandong secret police for months.

The state of human rights has quickly taken another turn for the worse, with the judicial system itself becoming a cruel force wherever citizens seek to uphold their basic rights. Citizens whose rights are violated now stand helpless. It is in light of the above, and the larger pattern of brazen, unlawful violations that China's citizens are being subjected to, that we hereby establish the Hunger Strike Group to Support Human Rights.

This is a group set against persecution and violence. Once fully in place, it will carry out symbolic hunger strikes in support of citizens who have encountered violence and wrongful persecution, be it inside China or beyond her borders. Such victims include workers, farmers, intellectuals, persons of faith, political figures, petitioners, democracy activists, army personnel, and even Party members and those in the public security system. Persons living abroad who have similarly been subjected to abuse—such as refugees from North Korea who have been mistreated by the Chinese government—will also be assisted.

We will offer support in the form of a hunger strike. It will be a hunger strike that makes no differentiation based on nationality, race, locale, religious belief, education, social status, or wealth. The format will be such that the hunger strike can be "relayed" from one person to the next, or one place to the next, as one would a hand-off. Members of the group can gather together in an appropriate place in their respective area (for example, in Beijing they could gather at the Shengzhi Law Office) and commence the hunger strike.

Each member of the group is to join the hunger strike for one day in his or her respective place. After the hunger strike has lasted a total of five days in a given area, it will then be passed along to another area, e.g., after the hunger strike has lasted five days in Beijing, it can then move on to an area in Shaanxi province. A daily journal of the hunger strike will be kept and published for the whole world to see. The support group will initiate the hunger strikes. Where a hunger strike is to be used as a method of supporting a designated victim, group members can relay the strike across various regions. The hunger strikes will circulate throughout the country nonstop until, finally, unlawful persecution ends.

When the support group has grown to a certain size, the group can adjust its form and location in order to respond to large-scale incidents, such as the recent shootings and persecution in Shanwei.

Whoever wishes to join the support group, please sign your name below.

Gao Zhisheng	*Ma Wendu*
Guo Feixiong	*Zhao Xin*
Hu Jia	*Qi Zhiyong*
Wang Guoqi	*Qian Yumin*
Ren Wanting	*Jia Jianying*
Yang Jing	*Li Hai*
Gao Jie (Japan)	*Teng Biao (via Gao Zhisheng)*
Li Heping (via Gao Zhisheng)	*Tian Yongde (Inner Mongolia)*
Du Daobin (Wuhan city)	

[The above is the original group of signatories, which launched the initiative. A great many others were to join the list soon after.]

Further signatures can be submitted to the website of The Epoch Times:

http://luntan.epochtimes.com/luntan/phpgb/index.php?topic=43

You can also send feedback and other signatures via email or fax:

talkdjy@gmail.com (China)
news@epochtimes.com (overseas)
Fax number: 1-917-591-2423

Responding to Arrests and Beatings

February 18, 2006

From 6 A.M. on February 18 through 6 A.M. on February 19, I will hold a hunger strike for the duration of the twenty-four hours in my Beijing office. My motivations are as follows:

First, this is done to support my compatriots who have suffered wrongful detention and persecution at the hands of China's communist regime simply for fasting in their own homes.

Second, it is to protest the communist regime's wanton affronts to basic human dignity and to what is commonly recognized in society as civilized behavior; it is to protest the regime's reckless disregard for China's constitution; and, it is in response to the same regime's severe encroachment upon my family's rights, carried out in the most obscene of fashions.

On mere grounds that I proposed hunger strikes to safeguard human rights, the communist regime has, over the past few days, resorted to crude and lawless means to persecute my family. Moreover, a large number of initial hunger strikers have been unlawfully arrested, detained, put under house arrest, and even physically beaten by authorities. On February 16, following the disappearances of Qi Zhiyong and Hu Jia, all three of my office's staff members were kidnapped by Beijing police. One of the three, Ouyang Xiaorong, had just come to Beijing to work for me as a volunteer and had scarcely been in Beijing twenty-four hours. His whereabouts are still unknown.

My assistant, the attorney Wen Haibo, was detained for over ten hours and is now under house arrest, barred from meeting with me. My home phone, office phone, fax, and Internet connection have all been cut off.

My entire family is being monitored and tailed by police twenty-four hours a day. We live under constant siege. Government authorities have shamelessly intruded into the private lives of my family!

In view of the current climate of terror, in light of the fact that hunger strike participants have suffered wanton persecution, and given that conditions necessary for me to coordinate the hunger strike have been stripped away, I would like to issue the following, urgent points outlining a new strategy for relay hunger strikes.

1. Starting today, I am going to hold a twenty-four hour hunger strike in my office every Saturday in protest of the violence being perpetrated;

2. In light of the regime's lawless and irredeemable actions, I suggest that from today on Chinese citizens spontaneously participate in the relay hunger strike and need not announce their phone numbers. They can furthermore use an alias when participating. Those who wish to use an alias should consider publishing remarks about the hunger strike or their personal journal entries. The relay hunger strike originally planned for Hunan, Shandong, and Guizhou provinces will be coordinated locally;

3. Every Saturday I will issue a statement with the names, some of which will be aliases, of hunger strikers who have decided to spontaneously join the effort;

4. I will initiate timely, nationwide hunger strikes whenever the communist regime uses bloody violence against Chinese citizens or whenever serious judicial or political persecution takes place; and

5. I wish to express thanks in particular to Mr. He Junren, a renowned attorney and member of the Hong Kong Legislative Council. Mr. He will hold a twenty-four-hour hunger strike every Wednesday in support of our hunger strike against violence. I hold him in great esteem.

Something Anyone Can Do

February 13, 2006

After over half a century now at the hands of the Chinese Communist Party, it is a final, tragic step that the downtrodden Chinese people have had to take: To use none other than our own bodies to say "No" to tyranny.

In 1989, we the Chinese people stepped forth from the comfort of our homes, using our own bodies in a peaceful and lawful manner, to demand that the nation's political system reform and become a democracy. The response from the communist regime was at once both astonishing and revealing. Namely, what we now refer to as the "Tiananmen Square Massacre"—a massive slaughter and roundup of those who were involved. That gruesome massacre showed the world the true face of China's communist regime. In the ensuing years, this regime has shown that it no longer cares about shame or moral values. If anything, it has become only more barbarous and ruthless, as evidenced by the torment to which it subjects its own people.

On February 4, 2006, we initiated a hunger strike in protest of the communist regime's tyranny toward, and persecution of, the Chinese people. As the hunger strike was taken up by Chinese overseas as well as in the mainland, our proposal was quickly interpreted as a brewing rebellion.

While the surging power of a hunger strike and the resistance it involves is indeed exciting, the decision to protest by means of a hunger strike is not something done with a joyful heart.

It's likely people do not realize that as of present, the regime has utterly lost its capacity to function properly when it comes to issues raised by the people. The reason behind this dysfunctional state is simple. From the day the regime seized power some fifty years ago all the way up through to today, it has never sincerely intended to ensure the basic dignity of a human being or the fundamental, common values of a society. Beyond having lost the ability to resolve problems, it has even empowered its malicious officials to—as bizarre as this may be—unscrupulously wreck its citizens' civilization, moral values, humanity, and basic legal rights.

Local governments often do the worst harm to the nation's citizens. Large numbers of victims thus look to the central government when justice is sought and basic rights are lacking. The central government, however, has no legal power to address citizens' specific petitions, and this fact alone spells tragedy for most petitioners. We therefore have a recipe for disaster in the incapacity of the central government to resolve things, the reluctance of local governments to resolve things, the abnormal demand for "stability," and the deceptive slogan "harmonious and flourishing society." The result is bloody violence and unlawful arrest of most all protesters and persons who dare to petition. The cruel persecution of petitioners in the post-1989 era is simply unprecedented.

China's communist regime has relied on forced labor policies for quite some time. The policies and their implementation are openly in violation of the constitution; a chief example is the unlawful detention of citizens who fight to safeguard human rights, or those who have religious beliefs. In recent years millions of citizens have been wrongfully detained solely on account of having a religious faith and exercising their right to freedom of religion. Today, millions of fellow Chinese are illegally detained in the name of "re-education through labor." The majority were protesters, religious believers, and those who petitioned the government for change using nonviolent means. The labor camp system has become a quicksand that innocent people must try to climb out of. While unlawfully detained, citizens are unable to obtain any form of legal representation and are left with no means to combat their unjust imprisonment. Citizens have simply no way to protect their rights.

Meanwhile, the unlawful and terrible persecution of democracy activists has reached absurd proportions. Across China, thousands of people are unlawfully detained, monitored, followed, and harassed. Beijing, Shanghai, and Guangzhou stand out as the worst offenders. Faced with feverish persecution from what can only be called sinister forces—most notably, secret police—victims once again have no avenues with which to pursue legal help.

In this way, ruthless government officials, using methods both obscene and barbarous, send an unmistakable message to the people: We are rogues, and we needn't obey the law; while you, the Chinese people, must choose between humiliation and death. Those who wish not to die or suffer in silence have but one other option: To use our own bodies to protest, via hunger strike, with the goal of changing this predicament in which we have no dignity. All workers, farmers, persons of faith, intellectuals, dissidents, Party members, government officials, soldiers, teachers, and foreigners who have been inhumanely tortured—one and all—can participate in this movement to safeguard rights. Each and every person can hereby find support when wrongfully persecuted. Therefore, so that we may carry out this aspiration with means both rational and nonviolent, I hereby propose a few suggestions for our hunger strikes, and wish to discuss them with our friends in China and abroad. They are as follows.

I. Any and all persons of conscience are welcome to join this hunger strike campaign that seeks to promote human rights and democracy. Anyone and everyone can participate in the effort, regardless of nationality, race, gender, beliefs, location of residence, income, or education. Everyone can support this movement, just as everyone can, in turn, gain protection from it.

II. The objective of the hunger strike campaign is this: to call on the Chinese government and its officials to abide by the constitution, by state laws, and by universally-recognized principles that protect human rights, civilization, basic human dignity, morality, and other common values. All Chinese and foreigners alike who have been wrongfully persecuted by their governments, or by officials who violate the above-said principles, can find support in this effort.

III. The hunger strike campaign to protect rights has been launched both inside China and beyond in synchronized fashion. Volunteers in each region are handling communications and plans there. Issues related to volunteer work within China are being handled by myself, Gao Zhisheng, as well as by Mr. Hu Jia, Mr. Qi Zhiyong, and other volunteers in various provinces and cities. They can be reached by telephone at 010-51630281, 010-86000663, and 010-86268964, or by email (for the time being) at mwd111@gmail.com. All who wish to volunteer for the effort may get in touch via telephone or email. Please be sure to provide your name, gender, nationality, phone number, email address, and other relevant information. If possible, please provide them with a brief introduction to yourself.

IV. The plans for the hunger strike are as follows.

Inside China, participants will be those who volunteer to join the effort, and the activity will be passed along in relay-fashion from place to place. The relay hunger strike will consist of two persons each day. The maximum amount of time for any given area is three days, after which the strike is relayed to another area. As for appropriate settings for the hunger strike, participants can go about it at home or other places they deem suitable. If possible, the two participants in a given area should do the strike together at the same location. Each relay hunger strike "shift" lasts twenty-four hours.

For those outside China, we urge such volunteers to maintain good communication with their counterparts in China so that overseas efforts can be counted as part of our hunger strike campaign. The ultimate goal of the activity is to set a model and precedent for larger hunger strikes that may be relayed around the globe in defense of civil rights. This will ensure the continuity and breadth of this nonviolent movement to defend human rights.

In the event of extraordinary circumstances—such as a massacre, large-scale violence, overt judicial persecution, violent abuse in prisons, or other circumstances, domestic or international, that the public deems major—the hunger strike may be launched in multiple areas across China simultaneously, rather than in relay fashion. A large-scale hunger strike might even be, in such cases, concurrently launched both at home and abroad.

During the course of the regular, relay hunger strikes, the names of any individuals or organizations participating in the campaign shall be clearly announced in the bulletin on that or the following day—with the exception of those not wishing to publicize their names.

V. Starting on February 15, the relay hunger strike campaign will publish a daily edition of the *Hunger Strike Bulletin to Protect Rights*. The bulletin's contents should include the following.

1. Names of persons who are to be supported by the hunger strike, as well as a brief summary of the facts of the unlawful persecution they have suffered.

2. Names of persons participating in the hunger strike that day; the location of the hunger strike; phone numbers of those who agree to publicize their names; and the names, locations, and phone numbers

of those who wish to participate in the relay hunger strike the following day.

3. Names of persons volunteering to hunger strike in other locations, along with their general information.

VI. If possible, hunger strikers should keep a "hunger strike journal" and make it public at some point before the individual's hunger strike ends; the format of journal entries is flexible. This will provide a vehicle for exchanging views and insights on the process and allow persons to articulate the reasons for their actions.

VII. The tentative sequence for the relay hunger strike will be, for starters, as follows: Beijing, Zhejiang, Hubei, Henan, Shaanxi, Guangdong, Shanghai, Jiangxi, Yunnan, Guangxi, Xinjiang, Hunan, Hebei, Sichuan, Shandong, Jilin, Liaoning, Heilongjiang, Jiangsu, Anhui.

VIII. If we believe that legal remedies are available to us, we shall determinedly use legal means in our attempt to defend human rights. As to cases that cannot be redressed via legal channels—such as the terrible crimes committed against individuals by the communist regime, at nearly every level of government, involving everything from local offices to ranking officials, and involving overt abuse of judicial powers—we will insist on staging a hunger strike as a form of protest. If someone is persecuted for joining the effort, a joint hunger strike initiative will be immediately launched around the world. In the specific cases of persecution against Mr. Hu Jia, Mr. Qi Zhihyong, and Mr. Qi Qinhong in Guangxi province's Qinzhou city (on account of their participation in the hunger strike campaign), we will launch a joint hunger strike when an opportune time arrives.

IX. The relay hunger strike effort to defend people's rights will last until China sees the establishment of an independent judicial system that can ensure the protection of people's rights. Under special circumstances, however, we may need to temporarily suspend the campaign; that will be done after consulting with various groups.

X. There are still a large number of innocent persons illegally incarcerated in China. For instance, at present many advocates of freedom and democracy are still subject to arbitrary crackdowns and persecution. Among the democracy and human rights activists still subject to unlawful jailing are Mr. Zheng Yichun, Mr. Yang Tianshui, Mr. Xu Wanping, Mr. Yang Zili, and Mr. Ye Guozhu. Some of them have repeatedly been victims of inhuman abuse while in custody. When the time is ripe we will address this situation with a hunger strike campaign and, by doing so, make a show of support for all who are persecuted.

Staying the Course with Nonviolence

February 21, 2006

I once wrote that a police state is naturally the enemy of the rule of law. Today's China is a full-fledged police state. In recent years, China's police force has operated more and more like a gang. The change is occurring so quickly it has shocked civilized societies. This is especially true in well-to-do areas such as Beijing, Shanghai, and Guangzhou. If we concede that China's police have all along been a gang-like group, then the evilness, brutality, and unscrupulousness of this group have come to a head in recent years.

With the police force having morphed as such, and with the justice system having now abandoned its task of protecting even people's most basic rights, millions of citizens have nowhere to turn when they have grievances. What's more, they have been deprived of the right to lawfully demand that abuses be stopped, say nothing of having perpetrators held accountable, just as they have lost the right to file complaints with petitions offices.

Worse still, citizens' attempts to exercise these rights have become fodder for cold-blooded local officials who suppress and persecute them. These officials no longer hesitate to kill citizens who resort to nonviolent means to fight for their rights. Such an affront to basic human dignity, and the yearning for survival it spurs, are truly outrageous.

In recent decades local authorities have used lies, violence, and other sordid means—such as unlawful arrests—as their principal means of preserving so-called "stability." Local governments now face a serious problem: No matter how fervent they are in their propaganda campaigns, people just don't believe their lies anymore, which drives these officials mad. For example, during this New Year holiday, I observed that in northern Shaanxi many farmers simply refused to turn on their televisions to watch the state-run CCTV's annual celebration. When asked why, they answered with honesty: "CCTV never tells the truth!"

The madness of it all has driven people to extremes; they see no other way to deal with a number of social problems and disputes. One representative of a group of petitioners said, "In the past, [local officials] might arrest us, beat us, and detain us on any grounds. But now the situation is such that they can arrest us, beat us, and detain us without any grounds."

In February 2006, I proposed to start a relay hunger strike in support of human rights. The initiative was born out of my ongoing concern that police are openly adopting gangster-like means, with basic human rights and legal protections being violently abused. My vision was to protest the police's harassment by starting a hunger strike—a nonviolent, moderate, and controlled form of resistance that would do harm only to our own bodies.

At the same time, I wanted to remind those running the system—that is, people who have never known the reality of things at the local level—that if the police's gangster-like actions were to not be stopped, China would soon be dragged into an abyss. Even though ours was such a restrained and small-scale resistance, and used as a last resort, what we nevertheless met with was yet more inhumane suppression by local police. The measures they adopted were even more deplorable and criminal than before.

All citizens who have participated in our hunger strikes have, without exception, been harassed, wrongfully interrogated, and subjected to intimidation by these thuggish police. Worst of all were events in Beijing and Shanghai, where all who took part in the hunger strikes were arrested without any grounds or due process. The brutish police's actions, insofar as they wantonly deprive people of their civil liberties, bear no resemblance to the lawful exercise of police power in normal states.

Even those experts and scholars who have shown sympathy for our cause have been unlawfully summoned and interrogated, their families subjected to constant harassment and police threats. For example, police harassed Dr. Fan Yafeng at his home multiple times each day, and even went so far as to harass his mother—repeatedly—despite her being a quiet old lady. The horribleness of these thuggish officers and those behind them defies description.

In light of this madness, seen in the police's ferocity and lawlessness, no small number of experts and scholars in China have advised me to stop the hunger strikes sooner rather than later. For their concern, I express my appreciation and understanding. Since I haven't the means to reply to each of them individually, I will share my thoughts here.

We are using moderate forms of resistance in order to protest the Chinese government's condoning of gangster-like police practices and, as a result, we have met with yet more intense persecution at the hands of the government. We have not seen the changes in circumstances that would prompt us to give up our resistance. If we were to give up now, it would mean we were abandoning the fight for basic human justice. It would also mean we were abandoning our innate right to defend basic human dignity, and were capitulating to the very renegade authorities that we protest. Police and authorities in China would then arrive, through perverted logic, at the conclusion that Chinese are best managed with gangster-like means, and that such means produce quick results.

The waves of hunger strikes now sweeping the nation stem from decades of uninhibited oppression by the authorities; they are not the product of any one individual's inspiration. The authorities, armed with their powerful machinery of oppression, know only how to silence people with coercion and violence, and do not understand—or do not want to understand—the importance of responding to the people's voice, let alone doing so with goodwill. I stand by my belief and I stand by these actions meant to stem the tide of violence. I will continue to do so until a change in the authorities' attitude takes place. I am prepared for any consequences.

What Would Heaven Want, Dear Brothers and Sisters?

May 6, 2006

We cannot fathom how the people of China continue to learn of their fellow citizens being tortured and murdered by Chinese authorities, yet still remain silent. Our relay hunger strike means to call attention to those who have been hurt by tyranny and are alone. Their ranks, we are coming to realize, are increasing ever more rapidly.

On May 2, a Christian in Harbin, of Heilongjiang province, called me to say that his church has been under attack from the Harbin Public Security Bureau. He revealed that police had arrested and detained hundreds of members of his congregation over the past year alone. Police there have apparently made it their profession to detain and brutally beat helpless Christians. They also steal money from the detainees and extort ransom payments from their families. Many are sentenced to long jail terms for vague crimes such as "illegal business operations" and "disturbance of social order."

On May 3, a Christian whose last name was Lu called me from Shenyang city to reveal how he and his son, along with other house church members, had been robbed by police from the Harbin Public Security Bureau's national security team. He shared that he and his son are evangelists. One day last year, while at a house church gathering, they unexpectedly fell victim to a violent police assault. Everyone present was unlawfully searched and robbed of their valuables. They were told that they would have to pay $3,748 per person or face imprisonment for an unknown length of time. Police told them, "Your crimes are very serious, and each of you may be sentenced to a few years."

They replied by saying that they were from Shenyang and didn't have that kind of money. "The police then escorted us all the way to Shenyang to ensure that they got their money," he said. "The following year, they had the audacity to return [to Shenyang] and extort even more money from us." Situations such as the one he relayed have grown quite common, and many like him are at a loss for what to do.

On May 4, I received a call for help from a petitioner named Song Guijia, from Liaoning province. He and his group of petitioners had marched to the Great Wall at Badaling, near Beijing, to call for human rights. Upon arrival the whole group was arrested. Song remarked, "We didn't break any laws—how could they arrest us?"

On the morning of May 5, the family members of Mr. Liu Yuhua, a Christian from Linshu county in Shandong province, called me for help. They told me that Liu had been arrested on the morning of April 26 on grounds of selling books related to Christianity. The Linshu County Police Department charged Liu with "conducting illegal business." Liu was then held in police custody. Liu's wife, who is also a Christian, told me: "Police not only looked into Brother Liu's bank account, but mine as well. They also ransacked his office."

Today I learned of similar news of Christians having been persecuted. In this case, two Christians, Mr. Lu Changping and a person surnamed Qin, both from Ankang city of Shaanxi province, were arrested during a house church gathering in Shiyan city of Hubei province; police stormed the group's gathering, in fact. My source relayed that the two have been held for seven months now in Prison No. 2 of Shiyan. "They were beaten harshly at the time of arrest, to the extent that both nearly lost consciousness," he said. "After being held for seven months, they have suffered enough."

In the afternoon, I received a message saying that Pan Zheng, a Christian from Jingmen city, of Hubei province, had been arrested for attending a house church gathering in Changde city of Hunan province. More than ten others were arrested with him, and have since been unlawfully jailed for six months in Changde. My source said, "Most of them have been tortured severely! Mr. Gao, if the persecuted Falun Gong can stand up and speak out the truth, why aren't Christians doing the same?" He went on to say that all of this was simply "too brutal, just too horrible," and that, "it cannot go on like this!"

Benjamin Constant once wrote:

> Religion touches all times, all places, all governments. Its sanctuary is the consciousness of man, and consciousness is the sole faculty which man can never sacrifice to a social convention. Religion will not lend itself to any association, any relation of supremacy or submission with political government... The political body must not have dominion over any religion.

Religion—something so precious—has become the target of the Party and its henchmen, and is something they madly seek to destroy. From the above, one can glean that the viciousness of their completely irrational persecution has now gone beyond the Party's own need to deprive people of freedom of belief, a need which is rooted in the Party's wicked autocratic nature. The apparatus of persecution now serves as a private weapon for those wicked Party members who have no conscience, for through it they extort and rob the victims. It's time people woke up!

The situation of Christianity in China is akin to that of the eight supposed "democratic parties" of China, all of which are controlled by the Party. The Three-Self Patriotic Movement Committee of the Protestant Churches of China, the Catholic Patriotic Church, and other state-sanctioned religious groups are nothing but pawns of the regime. Just look at Three-Self Church founder Wu Yaozong's own words: "God has taken the keys to salvation from the hands of the church and transferred them to the Communist Party." These Christian organizations have accepted the Chinese Communist Party as their god, and now serve to mask the Party's persecution of religious groups.

The Chinese Catholic Patriotic Association, meanwhile, is not much different from the Protestant Three-Self Church. Recently, the communist regime flouted Roman Catholic ordinances and opposition from the Vatican by deciding to appoint Ma Yinglin, of Yunnan province, as a Bishop. It is exactly this Ma Yinglin who has strongly advocated the persecution of house church members. Therefore, all of our brothers and sisters who believe in Jesus not only cannot place hope in the Party, but must also take the extra step of exposing the Party's guise of religious freedom (accomplished via pseudo-religious groups such as the above). This way, the international community might understand the ruthless persecution that we, who are true followers of Jesus and who carry the Cross, are facing.

Jesus said, "you who are cursed, into the eternal fire prepared for the devil and his angels," as well as: "For I was hungry and you gave me nothing to eat, I was thirsty and you gave me nothing to drink. I was a stranger and you did not invite me in, I needed clothes and you did not clothe me, I was sick and in prison and you did not look after me. They also will answer, 'Lord, when did we see you hungry or thirsty or a stranger or needing clothes or sick or in prison, and did not help you?' He will reply, 'I tell you the truth, whatever you did not do for one of the least of these, you did not do for me.'" (Matthew 25:31–46)

We must heed the teachings of Jesus, for we believe in the same Lord. Anyone who has been imprisoned at the hands of the Party because of his faith in Jesus, even if he is the least of us, must be the object of our care and concern. Outside of China there are nearly 2 billion people who believe in Jesus, such as Catholics, Protestants, and Orthodox Christians. It is our duty to inform them that our house church members are suffering persecution under the Chinese regime, and all on account of a willingness to love the Lord "with all our heart, mind, and strength" instead of loving the Chinese Communist Party. I don't consider this a political issue, for the power of Jesus transcends all nations on earth. His sacred power is absolutely not limited by any region, any political power, or any authority. Thus we shall unite under the name of Jesus and end the persecution. We can anticipate that America in particular—having been founded by Protestants—as well as the many European nations that boast many Catholic and Orthodox believers, will feel called to help us.

The greatest thing we can do for those suffering under this persecution is to do our best to end it.

From history we know that the Roman Empire eventually paid for its persecution of Christians. It had to endure three great plagues. Even after Constantine the Great recognized Christianity, the Roman Empire still had to bear the consequences of its previous actions. The western Roman Empire was destroyed by barbarian invasion, and the eastern Roman Empire, with the rule of the Byzantine Empire, survived over a thousand years longer than its western counterpart. I believe this was because the Lord blessed Constantine the Great's reign for his recognition of Christianity.

So you can see, to end the persecution of Christians is to have compassion for the perpetrators, in fact. By keeping them from shedding any more Christian blood, we attempt to save them from the fires of Hell.

Jesus said, "He that loveth father or mother more than me is not worthy of me; and he that loveth son or daughter more than me is not worthy of me. And he that doth not take his cross and follow after me, is not worthy of me. He that findeth his life shall lose it; and he that loseth his life for my sake shall find it." (Matthew 10: 37–39).

Facing the Chinese Communist Party's persecution of those who believe in Jesus, every Christian should have the courage to "carry the cross," as opposed to being numb to the suffering of fellow brothers and sisters.

Today, let us fellow Chinese hailing from twenty-nine provinces who have participated in the relay hunger strike to defend human rights every Saturday for the past several months, continue on for another twenty-four-hour hunger strike. We hereby show our support to those Christians, Falun Gong practitioners, and all citizens who are being persecuted under all kinds of false pretenses by the Party; we support these people no matter how many there might be! We hereby condemn and protest the continued tyranny, the corruption, and the inhumane persecution of innocent citizens. Each of us must be an agent of change!

Our Victories

March 2, 2006

Two more fellow citizens who came to Beijing to petition have died. The news came as I was eating. I quietly set my bowl down upon hearing it. They were killed while trying to escape from lawless police.

When they were alive, this communist system made their lives miserable. As if it wasn't bad enough that the system did them injustice, it dealt them further tragedy when they set out to reclaim their rights. And ultimately, it was the same system that "ended" their suffering in this world by ending their lives.

Every year before and during the National People's Congress and the National Political Consultative Conference, misfortune befalls many ordinary Chinese—especially those who come to Beijing to petition authorities. Every year around this time, large numbers of innocent petitioners, who come to Beijing ready to air their complaints to the supposed representatives of the people, meet with unlawful arrest, detention, and even torture. And as of yesterday, we have two additional deaths. These two were petitioners from Heilongjiang province. They were killed as they tried to sprint across train tracks, a train fast approaching, hoping to shake the policemen who chased them without grounds. Two other people were injured.

When the joyous "people's representatives" make their way to the conference hall, they walk on a red carpet stained with the blood and tears of an ever-mounting number of innocent, fellow citizens; this is particularly the case this year. Just two evenings ago, many petitioners who had hoped to find justice were arrested, and the blood of two dead innocent petitioners and the tears of their families—sacrifices to these unethical conferences—are additional evidence of the cruelty of this barbarous system.

Here, on behalf of my family, I would like to mourn the deaths of the two petitioners, whose names I still don't know, and to convey to their families our condolences.

The "people's representatives" to the two conferences should show some sign of humanity! You should observe a moment of silence—even if for just a few seconds—for the fellow citizens who came to you for help and died because of you.

Since February 15, my eyes have been blindfolded by the authorities but my ears can still make things out from time to time.

I have heard that people have been talking of late about the relay hunger strike that I started in support of rights and against violence and persecution, and it's said that those involved in this discussion are quite enthusiastic. I have even heard that a good number of folks are enjoying themselves a bit too much in such discussion, and some of them are always excited by it. One wonders if this is the only sense of fulfillment the relay hunger strikes have brought these people. I know little about these discussions, though, since I haven't been involved in them. All the same, I want to make a few comments on some of the remarks and challenges that have come up.

With regard to the personal attacks on Ms. Ding Zilin[1] that were heard in the discussions, that is simply unacceptable—regardless of who made those attacks or what the motives were. We should encourage everyone to speak up, rely on the strength of logic to persuade people, and adopt an opened-minded, prudent, and constructive approach, rather than hastening to show the dark side of man. No one should be condemned because of his or her words or thoughts. Words and thoughts pose a threat to no one. Just the opposite, it is precisely those who regard words and thoughts as a threat that are the real threat.

No one should, nor could, negate all the efforts, contributions, and sacrifices that Ms. Ding has made in this age of a twisted China; she has done a great service safeguarding people's basic human rights, human dignity, and our civilization more broadly. We share the same vision with Ms. Ding in that we seek to safeguard basic human rights and explore the value of freedom, democracy, and rule of law in China. No one should claim that his or her method or theory is absolutely correct. Those involved in the discussion can stand by their positions, but should not go so far as to impose their ideas on others not involved. Still less should they harbor any hope of getting others to support or oppose what someone is doing. You will either be disappointed at the outcome, or simply waste a lot of energy quarreling. That would defeat the very purpose of our initiative.

One opinion raised during the discussions claimed that our relay hunger strike is unclear in its demands, and that the authorities thus cannot answer its call. Another concern was that if authorities never acquiesce, our hunger strikers will find it awkward to end the strike.

The persons raising these opinions have narrowly defined the value of the relay hunger strike or what we might count as a "victory." In

---

1 Ding, who is known for her founding of the Tiananmen Mothers advocacy group, wrote an open letter critical of the hunger strikes that in turn provoked criticism of Ding.

other words, they're evaluating the success of this campaign in terms of tangible results: the authorities' response. This runs completely contrary to our initial purpose.

What defines our victories? If we, today, confronted with a regime that lacks a regulatory mechanism and moral norms, were to pin our hopes on the unreasonable government, we would end up with nothing and might even be put in a difficult predicament. With that approach we would never know victory.

Our relay hunger strikes have, in fact, achieved great victories. Consider the following:

First, a large number of Chinese people have stood up, and that is our victory;

Second, many Chinese have, on a scale that is unprecedented, courageously spoken out, and that is our victory;

Third, within an extremely short period of time, people from more than twenty provinces of China have joined in our effort, and that is our victory;

Fourth, our having exposed the barbaric tyranny, having raised people's awareness of the dictatorship, and having aroused a sense of participation is, in itself, our victory;

Fifth, our effort has furnished the outside, civilized world with an opportunity to observe and think about the political system and human rights in China, and that is our victory;

Sixth, our hunger strike campaign has provided everyone with a means to take part in a rights movement without having to leave their own homes, and that is our victory;

Seventh, in staging our hunger strikes we have used reason, self-control, and moderation, and that is our victory;

Eighth, within such a short period of time, democracy activists, human rights activists, petitioners, laid-off workers, land-deprived farmers, and persons from all walks of life have joined together in one movement, and that is our victory;

And ninth, by exposing the duplicity, ignorance, and savageness of the dictators, we have, with our effort, rendered them hysterical almost overnight, as shown by their cowardly and unlawful acts, and that is our victory!

Some people have accused the hunger strike movement of being naive on grounds that such activities were sure to irritate the authorities and goad them into doing wrong. But the very nature of the regime itself dictates that it will never cease doing evil. How could the blame be thrust upon nonviolent protesters? Is that logic any different from saying the reason that a hungry wolf wants to eat someone is because his flesh is so inviting? That is blaming the victim.

As of today, packs of secret policemen and shady thugs are still stationed outside my office. Petitioners and visitors from across China who have wished to see me have been—without exception—abducted, seized, and subjected to interrogation. Today alone, several visitors were arrested and interrogated. This afternoon, as I was on way to meet with a reporter from *The Times*, quite a police entourage was following me!

二天门

Since the writing of this book, the state-sponsored violence and intimidation directed at Gao and family have escalated. Gao was taken away by police in August 2006 and held in custody for three months. While in custody he was tortured. In December 2006, Gao was put on trial without his family or lawyer being notified and was, after being defended by court-appointed lawyers, convicted of "inciting subversion of state power." Thanks largely to international attention, his three-year sentence was suspended. Gao remains today under house arrest and is denied the right to practice law.

—Ed., June 14, 2007

Chronology of Gao Zhisheng's Life

1964 Born in a cave-dwelling in Xiaoshibanqiao village, Shaanxi province.

1975 Father dies. Lives with mother and six siblings. Gathers medicinal herbs in mountains to sell as support for poverty-stricken family.

1977 Starts middle school and attends for three years; must travel there by foot, one hour and a half each way.

1980 Passes entrance exam for specialized high school; cannot attend because of family's poverty. Becomes a coal miner.

1985 Joins People's Liberation Army and meets future wife, Geng He.

1988 Demobilized from the military.

1990 Marries Geng He, but couple must live apart for four years.

1991 Makes living as vegetable vendor in remote Xinjiang province. Learns of country's dearth of lawyers, begins to teach himself law.

1993 Daughter Geng Ge is born.

1994 Moves to Urumqi (in Xinjiang) to join Geng He and work in cement plant. Completes degree in law.

1995 Passes bar exam. Takes first case—a pro bono human rights matter. In ensuing years spends a third of his time providing legal aid to the needy and to victims of human rights violations.

1999 Wins largest amount of damages for medical malpractice in Chinese history, representing impoverished boy who lost hearing.

2000 Moves to Beijing and founds Shengzhi Law Office. Represents coal miners, businesspeople, evicted tenants, factory workers, religious believers, political activists, and others.

2001 Named one of China's top-ten lawyers following legal debate competition sponsored by China's Ministry of Justice.

2003 Son Gao Tianyu is born.

2004 Wins case for six factory workers from Guangdong province placed in police custody for having protested exploitation.

26 Dec 2004	Disregards government directives to lawyers by representing members of Falun Gong spiritual group.
31 Dec 2004	Writes open letter to National People's Congress detailing findings on state's persecution of the Falun Gong and violations of Chinese law.
7 Jul 2005	Represents Pastor Cai Zhuohua in court. Cai is sentenced to three years in prison for "illegal business practices," having printed and distributed copies of the Bible free of charge.
Sept 2005	Receives death threat after publishing exposé of government expropriation of private oil wells in Shaanxi.
18 Oct 2005	Writes open letter to China's Chairman and Prime Minister, calling for an end to suppression of the Falun Gong. Two days later, public security agents begin following and monitoring Gao and family.
4 Nov 2005	Beijing Judicial Bureau suspends Shengzhi Law Office's license for one year as retaliation.
10 Nov 2005	Letter is sent to George W. Bush from 138 organizations calling on Bush to raise Gao's case with Chinese authorities.

20 Nov 2005	UN Special Rapporteur on Torture, Manfred Nowak, meets with Gao while visiting China.
22 Nov 2005	Writes second open letter to China's Chairman and Prime Minister, describing harassment Gao and family were subjected to following October letter.
24 Nov 2005	Baptized; becomes member of Beijing house church.
29 Nov 2005	Evades security agents and travels to northeastern China to interview persecuted Falun Gong adherents. Spends 15 days investigating.
12 Dec 2005	Writes third open letter to Chairman and Prime Minister, detailing findings of investigation. Calls on regime to immediately desist its violent campaign against the group.
13 Dec 2005	Publicly announces withdrawal from Chinese Communist Party.
21 Dec 2005	Publishes investigative report on persecution of Christians in Xinjiang following on-site investigation.
11 Jan 2006	Establishes civilian fact-finding committee to investigate recent massacre in Shanwei city.

13 Jan 2006	Briefly detained by Beijing police after filming officers monitoring him. Warned by police that they could easily have him killed.
17 Jan 2006	Narrowly survives attempt on his life.
19 Jan 2006	Amnesty International issues "Urgent Action" appeal out of concern for Gao's safety. Three more appeals are issued in ensuing months.
4 Feb 2006	Initiates relay hunger strike for nonviolence and human rights, which quickly spreads across 22 provinces and to other countries.

The original Chinese book covered Gao's life up to this point.

The following are developments since that time.

26 April 2006	U.S. House of Representatives passes unanimous resolution in support of Gao, calls on China's authorities to "cease its harassment."
30 Jul 2006	Assaulted outside Beijing home by plainclothes police.
15 Aug 2006	Violently abducted from sister's home by plainclothes police. Surveillance of wife and children in Beijing tightens; they no longer may receive visitors.
Aug–Dec 2006	Held in police custody, cut off from outside world. Tied to metal chair and has strong lightsshone in eyes for a total of 590 hours (24 days).

21 Sept 2006	Chinese authorities issue documents charging him with "inciting subversion of state power;" family and lawyer are not notified of charges until two months later.
24 Nov 2006	Geng He is assaulted by police while shopping, leaving her hand and mouth bloodied.
6 Dec 2006	Granted "Human Rights Champion Award" by the Asia-Pacific Human Rights Foundation.
12 Dec 2006	Tried in secret by Beijing Municipal Court No. 1; neither family nor lawyers notified in advance. Defended by two court-appointed lawyers.
16 Dec 2006	Daughter assaulted by six police while returning from school, her back and thighs bruised.
22 Dec 2006	Court sentences Gao to three years in prison for "inciting subversion of state power." Afterwards suspends sentence for five years owing, observers remark, to international attention.
3 May 2007	Granted the "Courageous Advocacy Award" by American Board of Trial Advocates.
Present	Gao remains under house arrest, unable to practice law or engage in normal activities.